Juvenile Psychopathy

A Primer

2nd Edition

Jamie L. Flexon, Ph.D.

Second Edition: 2025

ISBN: **978-1-936651-23-8** (paperback)
ISBN: **978-1-936651-24-5** (ebook)

Printed in the United States of America

CONTENTS

Preface to the Second Edition

Few words in the American lexicon evoke such a powerful image in the minds of the public as that of *psychopath*. The word embodies those who commit atrocities often beyond what most can imagine. The condition, however rare, has captivated many because it is difficult to identify with people who seem to fail at having such base human traits that they seek to prey upon others without remorse, rather displaying a perceived satisfaction in it. While the term has become common and certainly overly applied, what this visage reflects is recognition that some in our society can commit atrocious acts against others without any perceivable amount of empathy. This is captivating because we simply cannot understand such a person, and yet we seek answers.

However tempting it is to throw around the label, psychopathy is a distinct clinical concept referring to a personality disorder that only applies when certain criteria are met. Adult psychopathic characteristics include callousness, lack of empathy and remorse, grandiosity, impulsivity, narcissism, among others. As noted above, it is a rare entity representing only about 1% of the population in general and 15 to 25% among the incarcerated according to some estimates (Dolan, 2004). Notwithstanding, as a result of the cultural meaning attached to the concept, many that seem to fail the empathy test or are involved with serious criminality get applied the psychopath label perhaps inappropriately so.

Much confusion persists on the topic. Mirroring this, one only needs to peruse the internet in a search of information about psychopathy to appreciate just how misunderstood the disorder is, and the amount of misinformation is striking, even from what would be typically considered legitimate sources. One article, quite erroneously, claimed that serial killers are psychopaths. Well, some are, but not

1

most. Another source declared that sociopathy and psychopathy are interchangeable, while others declare they are distinct. So, this depends upon who you ask. Yet another author lamented that psychopaths are necessarily violent, which is not always true. It seems that the more one looks around, the less clear is psychopathy.

Although some individuals may be misidentified as psychopathic, there is a certain type of hope that comes with misapplying the label. Since many have argued that psychopathy is immutable, if you only *look* like a psychopath, then perhaps there is a treatment. There may even be reasonable treatments for those with innate psychopathic features. Problematically, treatments are often considered only after some brutality is done and the psychopath label is applied, and by then, few want to necessarily treat such individuals. Quite the opposite, the public often demands a harsh and severe response. However, as with most things and as a thinking and sophisticated society, we must face this challenge as any other—with an eye toward pragmatism and hopefully prevention. The best place to look for such practical solutions is early on when characteristics of psychopathy are emerging, in efforts to sort out the who, the when, the why, and the response. Naturally, then, emergent or nascent psychopathy is where we need to investigate.

Toward that end, the first edition of this work examined psychopathy and, through extension, the recognition of psychopathy in youth. While the notion is still controversial, discerning the most appropriate ways to identify and measure nascent psychopathy is hardly settled. There are tendencies that show up in the research on adults and youth that offer clues that can inform risk and treatment.

This second edition expands upon that foundation. Since the original publication, some advances have taken place in the study of developmental psychopathy. Among the recent additions to this edition, refined youth psychopathy measures have been introduced (Chapters 1 and 2), and scholars have been working toward more precise assessments of secondary psychopathy, particularly as it relates to trauma and developmental histories (Chapters 3 and 4). The growing research on adverse childhood experiences (ACEs) has further illuminated potential origins of psychopathy and clarified pathways toward secondary-like variants (Chapter 4). The promise and limitations of different treatment strategies, including pharmacological interventions are also addressed (Chapter 4). Chapter 5 further advances more of the historical context of the psychopathy construct in the courts. In addition, an emerging body of research on epigenetics has added a biological layer to our understanding of how psychopathic traits may develop or become expressed (Chapter 6).

As with the first edition, what this work is not is an exhaustive review of the subject. It is still a primer in every sense, and much is intentionally left out. But this new edition takes account of these developments in an effort to update the conversation and provide a more complete view of the current state of youth psychopathy research.

Recognizing that there may be varied pathways to psychopathy is paramount to the discussion, because treatments cannot be realistically conceived without first understanding the underlying causes or contributing mechanisms of the condition. The research to date makes it reasonable to assume that there are multiple pathways to psychopathy (*equifinality*), and that some variants may be especially prone to aggression and violence while others may manifest in less overt but still harmful ways. This second edition especially emphasizes the growing recognition that psychopathy is not a single, uniform phenomenon but a constellation of developmental routes shaped by both biological and environmental influences. Epigenetic findings have begun to show

how early-life stressors can alter gene expression in ways that may heighten vulnerability, while research on adverse childhood experiences (ACEs) points to how trauma and neglect can carve distinct developmental trajectories. Together, these insights suggest that the origins of psychopathy are more dynamic and context-dependent than once believed, and that recognizing such variation is essential not only for theoretical clarity but also for crafting more targeted approaches to prevention, assessment, and treatment.

With that said, the orientation of this work remains one of simplicity aimed toward a broad audience. The deliberate curtailing of technical language is intentional. While some may prefer a deeper theoretical immersion, the goal here is accessibility, recognizing that the public conversation on psychopathy is too often shaped by sensationalism rather than science. The reality remains that, irrespective of the avalanche of research on psychopathy, including developmental psychopathy, there are more questions than settled empirical findings. Still, the progress of recent years gives cause for cautious optimism that the questions we continue to wrestle with may become clearer.

It is also worth recognizing here that it is one thing to be frustrated and excuse empirically-related issues for expediency and pragmatism in research. For those personally touched by this issue, there are real consequences. To those directly invested, I urge you not to accept the status quo that predicts that these youths are destined to a life of crime, parasitic lifestyle, and especially that there is no treatment for the manifestation of psychopathic-like tendencies. Research is ongoing, and the academic community is actively searching for meaningful answers.

CHAPTER 1

NASCENT PSYCHOPATHY:

AN INTRODUCTION

"The more I learn, the more I realize how much I don't know."

Albert Einstein

It should be noted upfront that this topic is not as strait forward as one might assume or prefer. It is best characterized as developing and informed by many different opinions. This is important to bear in mind when becoming oriented to discussions of juvenile psychopathy. This chapter will alert to some ongoing difficulties that will be further discussed in later chapters. The following provides a brief orientation to nest the remaining topics.

"Fledgling Psychopathy" and CU Traits

Quite obviously, people don't wake up one day as an adult and transform into the psychopath, but rather, psychopathic traits emerge early. In attempts to better understand psychopathy, scholars have turned attention to juveniles and preadolescents for clues to understanding *nascent psychopathy* (Flexon, 2016) with aims toward intervention and treatment.

Although scholars have recognized psychopathic features in youth for some time (e.g., Cleckley, 1941, 1976), Lynam (1996, 1997, 1998) coined the term *fledgling psychopathy* to account for the observed presence of what he believed to be psychopathic traits in youth. To him, hyperactivity, impulsivity, and attention difficulties linked with conduct problems were indicative of youthful psychopathy. More recent work has argued that there are a cluster of psychopathic features seen in youth that closely mirror that seen in adults, with Lynam and Gudonis' (2005, p. 381) more recent exploration into emerging psychopathy revealing that childhood and adult psychopathy bear high resemblance. This later understanding informs the current trends in identifying psychopathy in youth.

Currently, the features of juvenile psychopathy that have attracted the most interest center on being callous and interpersonally unemotional (CU traits), and it is specifically the presence of CU traits, that are counted as the hallmark feature of youthful psychopathy, which subsumes a lack of guilt (or remorselessness) and lack of empathy (Barry et al., 2000; Kimonis, Frick, & Barry, 2004; see also for discussion da Silva, Rijo, & Salekin, 2012). Very simply, being callous and interpersonally unemotional deals with such tendencies as not being concerned with the feelings of others, a lack of feeling bad or guilty about certain actions, and having blunted emotions.

Recently, however, some have made a case for moving beyond examining solely CU traits in youth. Salekin (2017), for example, argued for broadening the concept in youth from solely CU traits toward using the three dimensions of the psychopathy construct, namely CU traits in addition to grandiose-manipulative (GM) traits and daring-impulsive (DI) traits. This was argued to be important for moving beyond current limitations toward better identifying youth psychopathy. He also asserts that broadening the concept in this population will help clarify the dimensions of the disorder that appear differentially related to certain deficits and risks. Such a broadening of concept and disaggregation of features is further suggested to better inform the conduct disorder diagnosis linked to the Diagnostics and Statistical Manual for Mental Disorders (DSM) and the International Classification of Diseases (ICD) system and ultimately inform treatment.

While more discussion of the above points will be provided in the next chapter, it is important at this point to note the fluid nature of juvenile psychopathy. It is clear right away that defining psychopathy in youth is desirable; However, attempts toward that end continue to present challenge and change. Right now, identifying the presence of CU traits in youth seems the common approach for isolating emerging psychopathy, but many obstacles and a recognition of heterogeneity in research findings is leading to arguments to move beyond current practices. For the purposes here, the idea is that youthful psychopathy or emergent psychopathy is recognized by many and has been for some time. How to define and measure it poses problems.

Is Psychopathy Stable Over Time?

Adding to the idea that juvenile psychopathy exists is research examining the features of psychopathy over time. If characteristics of psychopathy can be identified in children and adolescents and these features persist into adulthood, then one can assume that there is stability or at least a degree of it. The research that has been conducted finds that central features of psychopathy demonstrate moderate stability from early childhood through adolescent years (e.g., Lynam & Gudonis, 2005) and from adolescence into adulthood (e.g., Lynam et al., 2007, 2008; Robins, 1966). However, not all identified as psychopathic early on retain the diagnostic label and some that did not have it as youth "developed" it later on. In fact, the numbers used to indicate stability (moderate and sometimes actually low) show something beyond the given purpose of the studies (see also Cauffman et al., 2016 for related discussion and findings on this point). That is, the issue is likely more nuanced than the question of whether psychopathy is or is not present over time. For example, Loney et al., (2007) examined anti-social and emotional detachment features of psychopathy in 16 to 18-year-old males and at six-year follow-up using the Minnesota Temperament Inventory (MTI), which is one of the earlier measures of psychopathy. The results demonstrated that the affective (emotional detachment) dimension of psychopathy was more stable than the anti-social (behavioral) dimension. Specifically, the authors note, "Not surprisingly, the adult transition was accompanied by a significant reduction in psychopathy scores, and the magnitude of reduction was greater for the Antisocial ($d = 0.67$) dimension relative to the Detachment dimension ($d = 0.49$). This is consistent with documented declines in antisocial behavior during the adult transition and, more specifically, with results regarding the antisocial dimension of the psychopathy construct" (Loney et al., 2007, p. 249).

The above indicates with little doubt that there is stability to varying degrees from childhood to adolescence and from adolescence to adulthood. The complimentary also is true; There is a degree of instability and depending upon which study is examined an impressive degree of instability is noted. It also appears that for different dimensions of psychopathy results are more nuanced.

The stability issue also alerts that there are problems with measurement accuracy and continuity of operationalization among scholars with respect to evaluating youth as with most areas of inquiry into juvenile psychopathy. Here, some of the measurement issues are attached to identifying and measuring psychopathy across age groups, such as using different conceptual measures and tools in attempts to match developmental age. Using aggregate statistics and related scores also obscures the ability to discern which children, youth or adults are moving toward or away from psychopathy. The bottom line appears to be that there is a degree of stability and its compliment, instability. As a result, consistent, absolute figures are not available and obscured.

Where Does Psychopathy Come From?

In tandem with the discussion over stability, scholars have sought to identify whether these characteristics are tied to genetic influence and have largely concluded that there is a genetic component, but also that environment plays a role (e.g., Larsson, Andershed, & Lichtenstein, 2006).

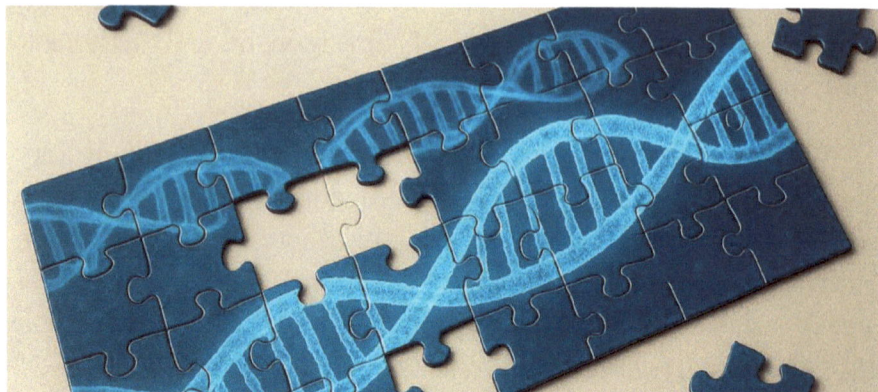

The work of Viding and colleagues (2005), for example, demonstrated a considerable amount of genetic influence on the presence of CU traits and anti-social behavior in 7-year-olds. Similar work, looking at dimensions of psychopathy in addition to CU traits has also found strong genetic influence for some of the traits making up the personality construct. In addition, others have found that genetic predisposition and unique (as opposed to shared) environmental influences are important to the development of psychopathy (e.g., Bezdjian, Raine, Baker, & Lynam 2011). Hence, the personality features revealed in at least some manifestations of psychopathy appear largely inherited, and now, it seems that there are certain aspects of psychopathy, such as those under the CU dimension specifically, that are the most implicated. On this point, one can also find research attempting to isolate the genes thought responsible for anti-social spectrum disorders and psychopathy, such as Monoamine Oxidase (MAOA) and the serotonin transporter (5HTT) gene (Gunter, Vaughn, & Philibert, 2010). However, this is emerging research, and more recent investigations have not appeared to move the conversation much further.

While psychopathy is most often identified in males (Vaughn & Howard, 2005), it also important to note that research demonstrates that these characteristics are normally distributed in the population (DeLisi, 2009; Edens et al., 2011; Murrie et al., 2007). This idea (normal distribution) is important as much less is known about psychopaths in the general population than that of forensic samples (those imprisoned/ or institutionalized). Such a reality leaves much left to explore. However, there has been a recent uptick in studies examining this area, e.g., Successful Psychopaths and in various non-forensic samples and contexts (see Sanz-Garcia et al., 2021 for review). So, what does all the above mean to practical understanding? At its base, we all have more or less of certain personality features. While for clinical pur)poses a youth may not be diagnosed with a personality disorder, the degree or level of personality features can be measured and are useful for treatment and research purposes.

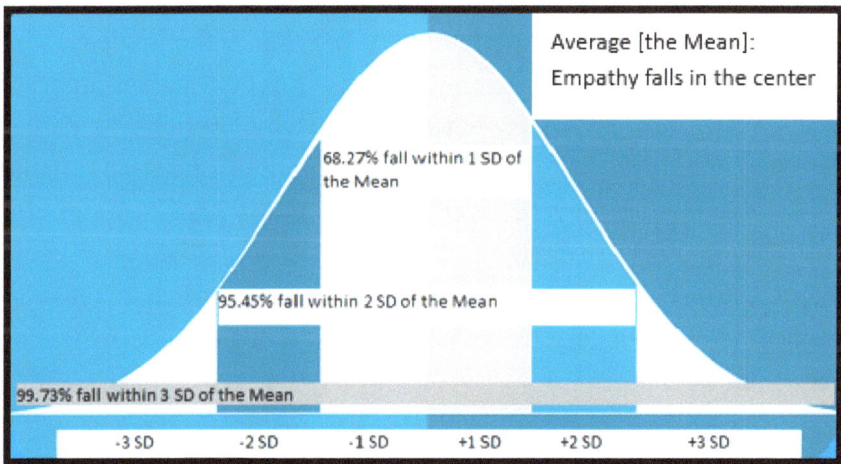

Figure 1.1. Normal Distribution Illustrating Empathy. Psychopathic values of empathy would fall well to the left of center into the negative values.

Figure 1.1 can be used to illustrate an example of a normally dis-

11

tributed trait or characteristic. Someone may show a high tendency to be empathetic or callous or any one of a number of characteristics. This person would appear to the right of center in the figure. The average person would fall somewhere on or near the center. The psychopathic individual would fall far to the left of center in the negative numbers. Such a trait may be inborn and then further cultivated or tempered by environmental influences.

Here, someone may simply be born with very low to no capacity to experience empathy in the same way most would expect. Does this mean that they are unavoidably bad? Not essentially, but it likely will mean that they process things in a way that few would immediately recognize or even identify as initially problematic.

Others also might misinterpret the responses of the low emotional or unempathetic person because people may infer emotional processes like their own. For example, when a small child watches a cartoon movie that features a sad event and the child doesn't react or responds without empathy, it may be overlooked as that's just how the child *copes*. One could even imagine that the child would be perceived as too sensitive and repressing their feelings. The point is that it may not be typical to immediately infer that the child is not experiencing emotions on par with others.

Similar processes are present with adolescent youth. Further, amidst what would be considered normal juvenile angst, certain adolescent tendencies such as impulsivity and narcissism have the potential to confound psychopathy assessments. This may present problems with identifying psychopathy in younger children and adolescents.

However, the recognition of extreme personality features ideally is paramount to clinicians and researchers. Also, it is important to note again that this does not mean that the youth will be necessarily prone to anti-sociality. While it does present as a risk factor, studies reveal that environmental factors are more often associated with anti-social outcomes. This point will be discussed in a later chapter.

Juvenile Psychopathy: CU Traits and Conduct Problems

Presently, most research concerning juvenile psychopathy either treats psychopathy as a homogeneous construct (e.g., Blais et al., 2014; Flexon & Meldrum, 2013) and/or involves offender or institutionalized samples (e.g., Kimonis et al., 2011; Vaughn, Edens, et al., 2009). Controversy also exists concerning whether the presence of conduct problems in association with high CU traits better predicts adult psychopathy than the presence of CU traits alone (see Fanti et al., 2013). However, the association between CU traits in youth, as a precursor to adult psychopathy, and volatile behaviors is muddied.

A number of researchers have linked CU traits with co-occurring conduct problems in childhood and adolescence. Some of the research suggests that the two are necessarily linked finding that the presence of CU traits predicts a more persistent and serious pattern of aggressive and anti-social behaviors (e.g., Frick, Ray, Thornton, & Kahn, 2014). This is in line with research using the construct to explain a number of malignant outcomes (e.g., Beaver, Boutwell, Barnes, Vaughn, & DeLisi, 2015; DeLisi, 2009; Flexon & Meldrum, 2013; Salekin, 2008; Salekin & Frick, 2005; Salekin, Neumann, Leistico, DiCicco, & Duro, 2004; Vaughn & DeLisi, 2008; Vaughn & Howard, 2005; Vaughn, Howard & DeLisi, 2008). This orientation of research persists, while others investigating CU traits don't necessarily connect them to aggressive, anti-social behaviors.

Given the extant research, it would appear that there is a relationship between the two, CU traits and anti-social behaviors, but it seems that the association may be complex or contoured and may be contaminated by the measures used to identify juvenile psychopathy, e.g., data and methods effects. To illustrate, when all types of psychopathic-like youth are combined, there is a clear statistical association with delinquency (e.g., Flexon & Meldrum, 2013). Although different types of psychopathy will be explored in another chapter, it's worth noting here that when researchers separate youth with psychopathic traits into groups, often called primary and secondary, those in the secondary group tend to show stronger links to antisocial behavior (Flexon, 2015, 2016). This offers a clue that there are youth with psychopathic features that are more implicated than others with anti-sociality. This is consistent with the literature on adult psychopathy (for review see Patrick, 2022). There are caveats to this point, but it is clear that scholars and clinicians need to note this distinction.

In addition to the delineation between variants briefly noted, research generally demonstrates that youth having solely CU traits do not necessarily engage in anti-social behaviors. This is important and it is worth repeating that for youth displaying conduct problems (i.e., conduct disorder), having co-occurring CU traits predict serious, persistent anti-sociality over having conduct problems alone (see discussion in Frick & Ray, 2015). As eluded to above, however, this persistent finding between psychopathy and anti-social behavior may also be related to how the construct is conceived and measured. Since about 50% of the most often used measure, which will be discussed in the next chapter, is made up of behavioral items, there is concern over the validity of some of the findings related to content overlap between the predictor and the outcome (Dawson at al., 2012, p. 65). This concern will be a continuing theme throughout this work.

How Many Psychopathic Youth Are There?

Discerning how many psychopathic-like youths there are is difficult owning to differences in the measures used to capture psychopathy and the varying populations (community, institutional) examined. For studies using behavioral items in measures used to identify psychopathy, it makes sense to use institutionalized samples as a means to capture a large population of psychopaths for research purposes. However, not everyone agrees with these measures and looking solely at institutionalized youth may miss those psychopathic-like adolescents that either avoid detection of their criminality or don't engage in it. As such, some studies examining psychopathic-like youth have specifically sought to look at the general population instead of institutionalized samples in efforts to identify and study any unknown or underappreciated populations associated with psychopathy.

For illustration, Figure 1 provides estimates from a community sample. The data are culled from the National Institute of Child Health and Human Development (NICHD)'s Study of Early Child Care and Youth Development (SECCYD). Note, the organization is not associated with this writing or any reported findings. The measures for the psychopathic-like youth (primary-like and secondary-like) are constructed from the Youth Psychopathic Traits Inventory's (YPTI) subscales of remorselessness, unemotionality, and callousness (CU Traits) developed by Andershed, Kerr, Stattin and Levander (2002) in concert with an anxiety scale to isolate those resembling the primary and secondary variants of psychopathy in the population of youth at large. Note, anxiety is often used to identify and differentiate variants of psychopaths (for review see Patrick, 2022 for related research findings).

The figure represents 3 categories: non-psychopathic youth, and primary and secondary variations of the disorder (variants). Primary and secondary psychopathic-like youth will be discussed later, but initially the primary type may be considered as (arguably) innately psychopathic, while there are more questions surrounding the etiology of the secondary type youth. According to this sample of youth taken from the general population, 20% would fall into the psychopathic-like category when using callousness and unemotional features of psychopathy and the presence or absence of anxiety for variant identification. This is a significant number, would counter the idea that psychopathy is rare, and reflects the difficulty of capturing the personality disorder in youth. If anxiety is excluded as a defining feature of psychopathy (primary youth), which aligns more with the adult conceptions of the disorder, then the estimate of psychopathic youth is 4.8%.

Obviously, the numbers of psychopathic youth presented in Figure 1.2 is greater than the estimate provided earlier (Preface) that indicated that psychopaths only represent 1% of the general population. Several reasons may underlie the discrepancy. It may be that the 20% figure (or 4.8% of the primary group) is capturing some of the dark figure of undercounted psychopaths (I refer to this as the *dark figure of psychopathy*), but it may also be that youth demonstrate a number of tendencies that may map onto the measurement scheme for psychopathy. There is also reasonable evidence that youth may grow out of some of the characteristics that would count them as psychopathic by some measures, which is demonstrated in the stability research. Youth who are dissociative may also be captured by measures aimed at psychopathy, which would result in them being included under the umbrella of psychopathic-like. It is equally plausible that the 1% estimate of psychopathy is incorrect or an underestimate because of reasons associated with measurement and conception.

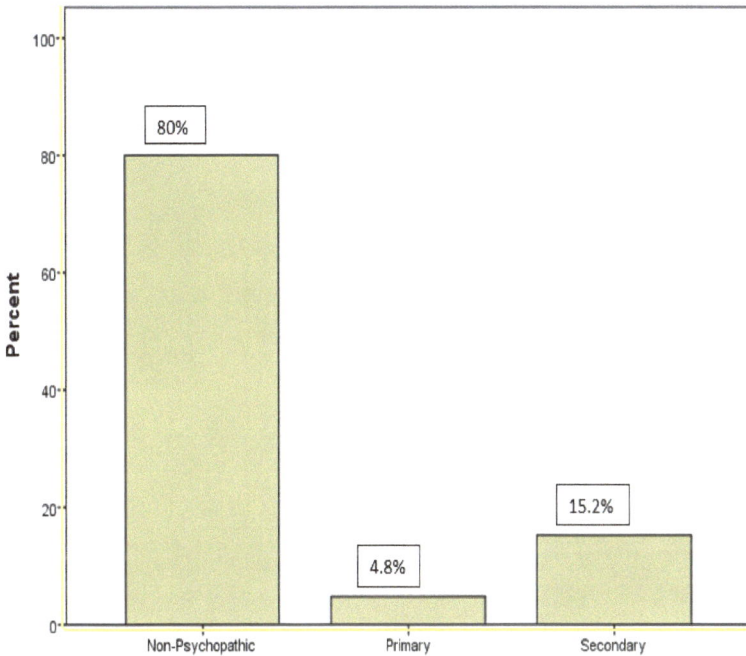

Figure 1.2. Distribution of Non-Psychopathic and Primary and Secondary Psychopathic-Like Youth in General Population Sample (N = 1,364).

Concerning the notion that some characteristics of youth may map on to certain features of psychopathy, yet be a part of normal development (e.g., narcissism, impulsivity); While these concerns manifest in discussions among scholars, there are those that believe such apprehensions are exaggerated (Lynam & Gudonis, 2005) as clinicians should be able to distinguish normal development from features of psychopathy (Michonski & Sharp, 2010, p. 6). However, not all clinicians are created equal, and it is not uncommon for a single individual to receive a different diagnosis depending upon which specialist is seen. Assuming that all clinicians are created equal, then, may be in error. Just as problematic would be going to a clinician who may over-diagnose juvenile psychopathy. Complicating matters further, given an accurate diagnosis, how would such youth be offered treatment? How would others, institutions, officials respond to such a youth?

Owning to the above, controversy surrounds applying the psychopath label to youth. Beyond social concerns over labeling someone a psycho-path and all the negative connotations that come along with it, how might a youth respond to receiving such a label or some synonymous condition with similar connotations? In the age of internet searches, access to diagnostic information certainly allows one to connect the dots. Imagine a 13-year-old youngster saddled with a diagnosis of psychopath or the age equivalent. Do they succumb to the label? Was it even justified given what we know about adolescent development? What images fill their mind in a society that vilifies psychopaths as serial killers and mass murderers and regularly and erroneously portrays them in popular entertainment programming?

Parents of youth facing a possible diagnosis of emerging psychopathy must also tackle an obviously emotional and challenging dilemma. They too are likely confronted with troubling images, and if a specialist is found, no standard treatment, at present, exists. Against such a backdrop, making choices about the care of their child is significant-

ly limited, while the consequences have the potential to be quite serious.

Problematically, there are a number of parents of psychopathic-like youth that aren't loving, available, competent or effective and are even abusive. A number of these parents are also tackling substance abuse problems. For some youth, these types of parents are argued to contribute to the psychopathy or the externalizing behaviors associated with it. Having such parents also would likely preclude or interfere with securing assistance. Given the above, the role of parenting as a risk factor and point of intervention will be discussed in subsequent chapters as will emerging research on treatments.

The following chapter, however, will cover conceptual development and definition of juvenile psychopathy, as well as measurement issues in more detail. While these ideas were briefly discussed here, there is certainly more to this conversation, and the issues raised in Chapter 2 will have a bearing on most matters discussed throughout this work.

CHAPTER 1 MAIN POINTS

❖ Individuals suffering from juvenile psychopathy are known to have a constellation of problematic characteristics that mirror that seen in adults.

❖ Early psychopathic-like traits show some stability over time and carry over into adulthood, while others seem to age-out (states).

❖ Psychopathic traits in youth (and adulthood) are associated with poor behavioral outcomes.

❖ There appears to be a genetic and environmental component to psychopathy.

❖ The essential feature(s) of juvenile psychopathy are argued to be CU traits, remorselessness and lack of empathy.

❖ Early traits initially may be missed.

❖ Identifying and labelling a youth with psychopathy can be inherently damaging.

CHAPTER 2

DEFINING AND MEASURING

JUVENILE PSYCHOPATHY

Defining Psychopathy

Discerning who is the nascent or emerging psychopath is obviously tied to how the concept is defined. Unfortunately, this fundamental issue is tied to debate in the literature so offering a strait forward definition is complicated. As some have argued, and rightfully so, the most common measures for psychopathy are operating in a theoretical vacuum and the measures have been confused with the construct (Skeen & Cooke, 2010). Indeed, it is troubling to repeatedly read that this or that measure has been used to define the construct. This is the opposite of how this should work, as the construct should inform the measure.

Little ground in conceptually defining psychopathy will be made as long as clinicians and researchers continue to move forward as though this issue has been resolved.

Since some claim to use the observations of Hervey Cleckley, M.D. to inform their work and measures, it seems prudent to go to the source when discerning the features of psychopathy. Through several editions of Cleckley's seminal work, *The Mask of Sanity*, the concept of psychopathy was refined. In his fifth edition, Cleckley (1976, p. 338-339) offers the following:

> *Before going on to the perhaps still unanswerable questions of why the psychopath behaves as he does or of how he comes to follow such a life scheme, let us, as was just suggested, attempt to say what the psychopath is in terms of his actions and his apparent intentions, so that we may recognize him readily and distinguish him from others.*
>
> *We shall list the characteristic points that have emerged and then discuss them in order:*
>
> *1. Superficial charm and good "intelligence"*
>
> *2. Absence of delusions and other signs of irrational thinking*
>
> *3. Absence of "nervousness" or psychoneurotic manifestations*
>
> *4. Unreliability*
>
> *5. Untruthfulness and insincerity*
>
> *6. Lack of remorse or shame*

7. Inadequately motivated antisocial behavior

8. Poor judgment and failure to learn by experience

9. Pathologic egocentricity and incapacity for love

10. General poverty in major affective reactions

11. Specific loss of insight

12. Unresponsiveness in general interpersonal relations

13. Fantastic and uninviting behavior with drink and sometimes without

14. Suicide rarely carried out

15. Sex life impersonal, trivial, and poorly integrated

16. Failure to follow any life plan

Cleckley's work references youth repeatedly when presenting case studies for illustrative purposes. This makes obvious sense as he regards psychopathy as a personality disorder that necessarily manifests from an early age, and he ties these case studies back to the characteristic list.

As noted, since the final iterations of Cleckley's book, a number of scholars have turned to his conceptual formulation of psychopathy. However, there is clear departure over time. This can be traced to difficulties in conceptually defining some of the characteristics he proposed and the DSM, which was created by the American Psychiatric Association, which uses behavioral indicators to diagnose anti-social personality disorder (ASPD). It is important to note, without getting too far off track, that psychopathy and ASPD were treated as one in the same in the DSM, and Cleckley treated them as synonymous. He specifically refers to the changing nomenclature of the American Psychiatric Association from the first edition of his book to the fifth edition in noting (Cleckley, 1976, p. viii):

> *The classification of psychopathic personality was changed to that of sociopathic personality in 1958. In 1968 it was changed again to antisocial personality. Like most psychiatrists I continue to think of the people who are the subject of this book as psychopaths and will most often refer to them by this familiar term. Sociopath or antisocial personality will sometimes appear, used as a synonym to designate patients with this specific pattern of disorder.*

Under current criteria, a youth may not be diagnosed with psychopathy and or ASPD as the individual must be aged 18 to formally receive the official diagnosis. This does not mean that it isn't happening, though reserving such a designation should be avoided. Acquiring the psychopath label, even informally and especially among youth, can have catastrophic ramifications and delay the implementation of strategies aimed at ameliorating any associated problems that may or may not belong to being a psychopath. Further, and related to the above, failing to accurately identify the psychopathic individual creates a situation whereas clear, well-defined characteristics are not appreciated, and more and more individuals are added to the ranks of those that can be included as being psychopathic because of the varied criteria. This makes it very difficult to isolate treatment protocols.

Fundamentally, the question becomes whether you are treating a psychopathic individual or someone that resembles a psychopathic individual. Some may believe that this is not an issue if the end result *looks* the same. However, looks can be deceiving. Here, a youth may be dissociating from early trauma and or having behavioral problems and overtly look like a psychopath. Is this youth a psychopath? Is there a differential feature? This potential for confounding is important to recognize. In essence, are you really addressing intrinsic shallow affect and lack of empathy or are you addressing dissociation and more externalizing behaviors, such as juvenile delinquency? Such features are indicators of psychopathy in the most common measurement tool, and as noted above, there is real concern that we are conflating the definition of the concept with the measurement (Skeem & Cooke, 2010a, 2010b).

Is Criminal Behavior a Discerning Feature of Psychopathy?

A common inclination is to use behavioral measures, in part, to define psychopathy along with the affective dimensions, such as CU traits. This often appears as an artifact of measurement schemes and is the most recognized in the literature and in practice. It has been argued, however, that it results in capturing an all too inclusive group of people that may be subjected to the label. Very simply, doing certain behaviors, particularly anti-social and criminal ones, may not be a sensitive enough indicator for psychopathy, and as one scholar fittingly notes, criminal or analogous behavior is neither necessary or sufficient to apply a psychopathy label (Veal & Ogloff, 2022). This is important and there are real world consequences. The label of psychopathy carries with it very negative overtones along with a belief that it is resistant to treatment. In *The Mask of Sanity*, Cleckley differentiates the psychopath from the typical criminal (1976, p. 261-267) and from other character and behavior disorders, including delinquency (1976, p. 267-272).

> *Many people, perhaps most, who commit violent and serious crimes fail to show the chief characteristics which so*

consistently appear in the cases we have considered. Many, in fact, show features that make it very difficult to identify them with this group. The term psychopath (or antisocial personality) as it is applied by various psychiatrists and hospital staffs sometimes becomes so broad that it might be applied to almost any criminal... I (comment omitted) maintain that the large group of maladjusted personalities whom I have personally studied and to whom this diagnosis has been consistently applied differs distinctly from a group of ordinary criminals. The essential reactive pattern appears to be in many important respects unlike the ordinary criminal's simpler and better organized revolt against society and to be something far more subtly pathologic. It is my opinion that when the typical psychopath, in the sense with which this term is here used, occasionally commits a major deed of violence, it is usually a casual act done not from tremendous passion or as a result of plans persistently followed with earnest compelling fervor. There is less to indicate excessively violent rage than a relatively weak emotion breaking through even weaker restraints. The psychopath is not volcanically explosive, at the mercy of irresistible drives and overwhelming rages of temper. Often he seems scarcely wholehearted, even in wrath or wickedness.

-See 1976, p. 262-263

The first point that Cleckley makes here is an important one. Concerning behavior, juvenile delinquency or anti-sociality may manifest in many conditions and situations without the individual having to be a psychopath. The behavior and other manifestations would be, essentially, secondary to some primary condition or circumstance. For example, a youth dissociating as a consequence of abuse may also engage in anti-social behaviors and bear essential resemblance to the psychopath, such as having impulsivity problems or other maladaptive coping mechanisms because of turbulent rearing. This individual may be responsive to tailored treatments because they possess the capacity to change. Whether an actual psychopath has the ability to respond to treatment is still in question and is the subject of a subsequent chapter. Failing to deal with this issue of definition and the resulting overinclusion will ultimately harm the ability to develop and evaluate treatment protocols.

The next point is equally important. The behavior is a manifestation of the personality, whereas there is a weak impulse met with weaker constraints over behavior. This lack of self-control does not necessarily translate into criminal behavior, but may certainly underlie anti-social behavior. Given this, disagreement exists among scholars about whether or not deviant and or criminal behavior should be included as an indicator or dimension of psychopathy (e.g., Hare & Neumann, 2010; Skeem & Cooke, 2010a, 2010b). As noted, one side of the debate considers criminal and problem behavior central to the construct (Hare & Neumann, 2005), while others contend that deviant and ''criminal behavior is an epiphenomenon that is neither diagnostic of psychopathy nor specific to personality deviation'' rather, criminal and violent behavior, in particular, is viewed as a later, downstream correlate of psychopathy (Skeem & Cooke, 2010a, p. 433). As discussed, this later position strongly echoes early theorizing about the character of psychopathy.

Cleckley's (1941) conception of successful and unsuccessful psychopaths over 70 years ago was largely informed by examining noninstitutionalized subjects, whereas those meeting the criteria of being egocentric, irresponsible, and using superficial charm were not necessarily criminal or institutionalized and were considered high functioning (Gao & Raine, 2010). He also recognized the tension that presented with using juvenile delinquency and criminality in youth for diagnostic purposes. Cleckley noted (1976, p. 270):

> *Confused manifestations of revolt or self-expression are, as everyone knows, more likely to produce unacceptable behavior during childhood and adolescence than in adult life. Sometimes persistent traits and tendencies of this sort and inadequate emotional responses indicate the picture of the psychopath early in his career. Sometimes, however, the child or the adolescent will for a while behave in a way that would seem scarcely possible to anyone but the true psychopath and later change, becoming a normal and useful member of society. Such cases put a serious responsibility on the psychiatrist.*

At the same time, Karpman (1941, 1948) argued that many being labeled with psychopathy were being ascribed so inappropriately. Karpan (1941) very sharply criticized this tendency to label those exhibiting anti-social behavior as a part of the diagnostic criteria for psychopathy because similar behavior can be tied to a plethora of disorders including bipolar disorder, schizoid disorders, metabolic disturbances, to name a very few. In essence, by including deviant/criminal behavior within the construct (as well as a number of other traits he dismisses), the label of psychopathy was being inappropriately applied since any number of psychic and medical disturbances could manifest with problem, abhorrent behavior. Thus, virtually any condition that co-manifested with aggression, violence or behavioral outbursts could result in misapplying psychopathy, leading to a great amount of over-inclusion. Hence, it was through such a lens that Karpman (1948) further clarified his discussion of heterogeneity in psychopathy, which will be discussed in another chapter. The point is that not all individuals with psychopathic personality features are violent, aggressive or engage in criminal behavior, (e.g., Cleckley, 1941; Flexon, 2015, 2016). This issue is augmented when considering youth for whom anti-social behavior and or delinquent acts become, to some extent, more normative through adolescence (e.g., age-crime curve, see Figure).

Relationship between Offender's Age and Arrest Rate

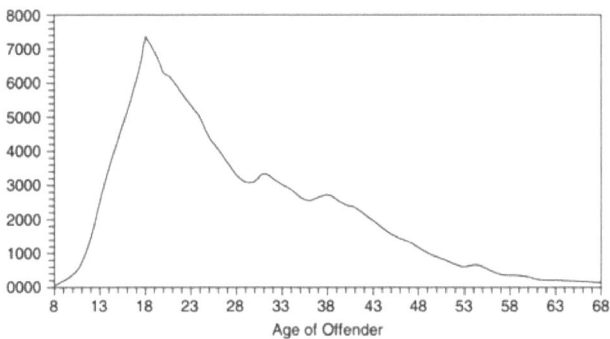

Notes: Arrest rate is per 100,000 age-specific population. Ages 00-08 are excluded from the figure because they account for an insufficient number of cases.

Figure 2.1. Example Age-Crime Curve. Provided with author permission from Stolzenberg and D'Alessio (2008).

What is juvenile psychopathy, then? It depends on who you ask. It would seem prudent, since we are talking about the manifestation of a personality disorder, to restrict the definition to characteristics that are consistent with the level of core, individual personality features that are essential to the disorder. According to some scholars and in deference to theorists, such features would include traits of emotional detachment, such as callousness, shallow affect, remorselessness, lack of empathy, egocentricity, and low trait anxiety (for discussion see

Skeem & Cooke, 2010a, p. 436). A differential feature may be the presence or absence of anxiety. While some use this presence of anxiety to differentiate between primary or secondary psychopathy, which will be discussed later, it may be that this feature can alert us to whether we are dealing with a psychopathic individual or one better included under the criteria for some other co-morbid condition. This idea will become clearer when discussing heterogeneity in psychopathy.

So, the definition of psychopathy remains elusive as it is entangled in scholarly camps, which is even more complicated when it is extended to youth. For clinical purposes, and irrespective of whether the diagnosis can be made to anyone under 18-years-old, there is obvious deference to the DSM, and many accept the status quo to further clinical and research objectives. Others remain committed to sorting through this fundamental obstacle of definition. Ironically, taking stock of the literature results in more questions concerning which findings are accurate, artifact of measurement, relevant, and or comparable. Since youth are the concern here, it is worth emphasizing (again) that it is quite normative for juveniles to engage in anti-social behaviors (i.e., age-crime curve) and environmental exposures can shape the form of that behavior. Since a number of youth who score as psychopathic on current, common measures also seem to age-out of their psychopathy, then more attention clearly needs to be paid to how we are measuring psychopathy, particularly in youth.

Measuring Psychopathy

Joining behavior to the construct of psychopathy can be traced back to early attempts at creating measurement tools to screen for psychopathy. This is the case with Hare's Psychopathy Checklist (PCL) and its modifications (Hare, 1991, 2003). Robert Hare's influence is undeniable in how psychopathy is conceived and his measure(s) represents the most commonly used method for screening psychopathy in adults and youth.

Hare's (1991, 2003) interview-based survey was aimed at largely forensic samples among criminal offenders, which underscores his inclusion of criminal and anti-social behaviors in the measure (Psychopathy Checklist, PCL; PCL-Revised, PCL-R; & PCL: Youth Version, PCL:YV). This was an attempt to operationalize Cleckley's early conception of psychopathy and others, while being attentive to the classification criteria set in place by the American Psychiatric Association for Antisocial Personality Disorder (ASPD).

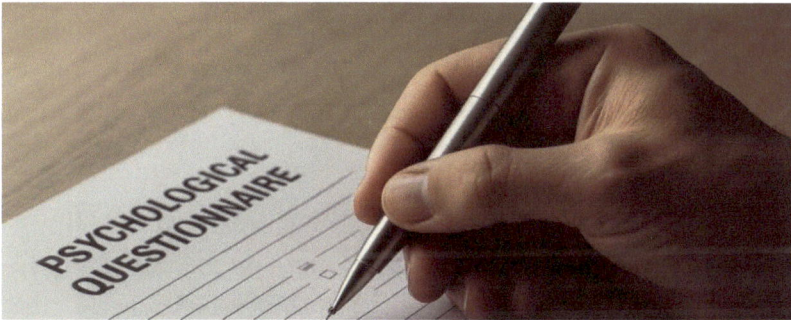

Hare's website describes the PCL:YV measure:

> *Identifying youth with psychopathic traits is critical to understanding the factors that contribute to the development of adult psychopathy. The Hare Psychopathy Checklist: Youth Version (PCL:YV) is a 20-item rating scale for the assessment of psychopathic traits in male and female offenders aged 12 to 18.*
>
> *Adapted from the Hare Psychopathy Checklist-Revised (PCL-R), the most widely used measure of psychopathy in*

*adults, the PCL:YV uses an expert-rater format that empha-
sizes the need for multidomain and multisource information.
Using a semi-structured interview and collateral information,
the PCL:YV measures interpersonal, affective, and behavioral features related to a widely understood, traditional concept
of psychopathy. The PCL:YV yields dimensional scores for
clinical purposes, but it can also be used to classify individuals into groups for research purposes.*

http://www.hare.org/scales/pclyv.html

The youth version of the measure is based on the PCL-R, which
clearly clings to the idea that behavior is to be included in defining
psychopathy as noted in the excerpt above. However, Cleckley's conception of psychopathy, for which Hare's measure partly relies upon,
does not treat criminality as a defining feature of psychopathy -but rather a rare exception that in itself is not a necessary manifestation of
the condition.

The following gets a bit technical to those less scientifically inclined, but is worth discussing nonetheless. Initially, measurement research exploring the factor structure of the of the PCL-R revealed that
there was at least a two-factor presentation. The first factor, *affective-
interpersonal* (factor 1), refers to those lacking empathy and remorse,
but having characteristics of being superficial, glib, narcissistic, and
being deceitful and manipulative; The second factor, *socially deviant
life-styles and behaviors* (factor 2), is connected to impulsivity, irresponsibility, low self-regulation,   early conduct problems, and adult
anti-social behavior (Harpur, Hare, & Hakstian, 1989; Hare et al.,
1991; see Bezdjian, Raine, Baker, & Lynam, 2011). Yet, other investigators have found three–*arrogant and deceitful interpersonal style,
deficient affective experience,* and *impulsive and irresponsible behavior* (Cook & Michie, 2001) and four factor solutions when examining

the construct–*Interpersonal, Affective, Lifestyle*, and *Anti-social* (Hare & Neumann, 2005). Such explorations tap into ongoing controversies in the literature.

From the original instrument, Factor 1 (Facet 1 = interpersonal; Facet 2 = affective) of Hare's PCL-R measure largely deals with the affective dimensions of psychopathy, see summary Table 2.1. Facet 1 (interpersonal) considers characteristics of being superficial and glib, having a grandiose self-worth, pathological lying, and being manipulative. Facet 2 entails lacking guilt or remorse, having a shallow affect, demonstrating a failure to accept responsibility, and being callous and lacking empathy. Factor 2 (Facet 3 = lifestyle; Facet 4 = anti-social) includes the behavioral dimension. Facet 3 includes indicators measuring stimulation-seeking, impulsivity, irresponsibility, lack of realistic goals, and parasitic lifestyle. The last facet, Facet 4, deals with identifying poor behavioral controls, early behavior problems, juvenile delinquency, revocation of conditional release, and criminal versatility.

As an aside and also worth mentioning is that the elements from Table 2.1 appear to represent a causal structure. For example, elements from Facet 2 (affective) can lead to the elements of Facet 1 (interpersonal). Elements of Facet 3 may underlie or be drivers of Facet 4 (anti-social) elements, etcetera. Of course, there would be back and forth on this point and expression of these traits (or states) might look different depending on developmental age.

Factor 2 items are most strongly linked with predicting anti-social behavior. For instance, in a large scale meta-analysis examining Hare's measure to anti-social behavior, researchers found that of the two factors, impulsive and anti-social traits predicted anti-social conduct more than the traits belonging to Factor 1, which was consistent with prior reviews (Leistico, Salekin, DeCoster, & Rogers, 2008, pp. 38-39). However, this is not shocking as behavior predicts behavior.

Theoretically, it is what is known as a tautology (also criterion contamination) and presents problems for trying to discern which innate features of psychopathy are responsible for any associated malignant behaviors. So, while much of the community persists in using Hare's PCL-R and its derivatives, there are concerns with its continued use because of the tautology issue and the large body of psychopathy research that relies on it to produce empirical findings that guide strategies for screening and treatment. Ultimately, since behavior is a manifestation of various mental processes, it cannot be uniquely nor neatly tied to any diagnostic criteria.

Table 2.1. Summary of Hare's Two-Factor Conception of Psychopathy	
FACTOR 1	
Facet 1 (Interpersonal)	superficial and glib, having a grandiose self-worth, pathological lying, and being manipulative
Facet 2 (Affective)	lacking guilt or remorse, having a shallow affect, demonstrating a failure to accept responsibility, and being callous and lacking empathy
FACTOR 2	
Facet 3 (Lifestyle)	impulsivity, stimulation-seeking, irresponsibility, lack of realistic goals, and parasitic lifestyle
Facet 4 (Anti-social)	poor behavioral controls, early behavior problems, juvenile delinquency, revocation of conditional release, and criminal versatility
Note: Modified from Glenn & Raine, 2014, p. 8, Figure 1.1.	

Trying to move beyond the measure would likely be met with a lot of inertia because of the persistent reliance on the PCL measurement tools for research and to inform the concept of psychopathy. The measure isn't supposed to define the concept, however. The concept is aimed at developing the measure; The measure is the operationalization of the concept. There are examples of back and forth on this point in the literature, as noted, and some scholars are devoted to studying this area relying on Hare's PCL-R for measuring psychopathy. Yet, developments surrounding new ways to capture the heart of the disorder have emerged in attempts to gauge psychopathy in non-forensic samples, i.e., the community at large, that attempt to avoid the issues associated with including behavioral indicators of psychopathy. Such sensitivity has resulted in the Psychopathic Personality Inventory (and revised version; Lilienfeld & Andrews, 1996; Lilienfeld & Widows, 2005) and the Elemental Psychopathy Assessment (Lyman et al., 2011).

A measurement tool that deserves discussion is the Comprehensive Assessment of Psychopathic Personality (CAPP or Comprehensive Assessment of Psychopathic Personality -Institutional Rating Scale CAPP-IRS; Cooke et al., 2004). The development of the measure given the current state of psychopathy assessment and research is laudable. The development of CAPP, in comparison with the PCL measures, was done to clarify the conceptual definition of psychopathy and to address identified shortcomings with other measures.

The developers of the CAPP used a bottom-up approach whereas a careful and thorough literature review was conducted, as well as a review of thoughtful clinical descriptions of the disorder by several experts. These reviews enabled the scholars to develop a list of psychopathy symptoms. Then, consultation with regard to the list was sought with subject matter experts for any agreement with the identified symptoms from the literature review. Modifications and additions of symptoms to the list were then made, and after the final list was devised, plain language, trait-descriptive adjectives or phrases were identified and used to consolidate the symptoms.

The approach yielded 33 symptoms, which were processed logically into 6 separate, functional domains of personality: Attachment, Behavioral, Cognitive, Dominance, Emotional, and Self domains (for further description of this process see Cooke et al., 2012). Table 2.2 summarizes the CAPP measure, which was constructed based on published information. Although the CAPP extends the bar in this area, which again, is certainly praiseworthy, some critical areas involve the potential to be over-inclusive, which the authors recognize as this was done intentionally. The authors also solicit feedback on the measure.

Examining, in particular, the behavioral domain of the CAPP, one can see that there may be some residuals owning to other measures, such as the PCL-R dominating the clinical and empirical landscape. It is not a secret at this point that there are heavy criticisms with the PCL incorporating, for example, anti-social and or criminal behaviors into the measure for the personality disorder of psychopathy. This reliance is also in keeping with the DSM criteria for ASPD. Recall, psychopathy and ASPD are often used interchangeably.

The CAPP retains the behavioral domain with less reliance on criminality. However, this persistence with using a behavioral domain in the CAPP that contains elements of aggression and violence may reflect the heavy reliance on forensic samples in the literature, which often uses the PCL for screening psychopathy. In concert with this reality is the use of clinical practitioners as subject matter experts to inform the CAPP who deal with behaviorally problematic clients and often have training in the PCL-R.

Since the literature and identification of psychopathic individuals relies on using perhaps problematic measures, what is known about this population is, to some extent, pre-determined. In that way, some of the noise from other measures can be contaminating present attempts to define the construct using a bottom-up approach. It may be that there is a population of individuals that aren't aggressive, violent, nor bear the behavioral symptoms as described in the measure, e.g., successful psychopaths. As an aside, in terms of extending the measure

to youth, parents of teenagers may find the list of plain language de-
scriptors in Table 2.2 alarming as they consider the characteristics of
their adolescent child. Developmental psychology has long recognized
that adolescents often appear self-absorbed (or even narcissistic),
which can be understood as part of *adolescent egocentrism* (Elkind,
1967). Many of these same characteristics resemble features listed in
Table 2.2; however, in adolescence they typically remain within the
subclinical range, reflecting normative development rather than diag-
nostic-level pathology.

Table 2.2. Comprehensive Assessment of Psychopathic Personality (CAPP) Psychopathic Domains and Symptoms	
SELF	
self-centered	egocentric, selfish, self-absorbed
self-aggrandizing	self-important, conceited, condescending
sense of uniqueness	sense of being extraordinary, exceptional, special
sense of entitlement	demanding, insistent, sense of being deserving
sense of invulnerability	sense of being invincible, indestructible, unbeatable
self-justifying	minimizing, denying, blaming
unstable self-concept	labile, incomplete, chaotic sense of self
EMOTIONAL	
lacks anxiety	unconcerned, unworried, fearless
lacks pleasure	pessimistic, gloomy, unenthusiastic
lacks emotional depth	unemotional, indifferent, inexpressive
lacks emotional stability	temperamental, moody, irritable
lacks remorse	unrepentant, unapologetic, unashamed
DOMINANCE	
antagonistic	hostile, disagreeable, contemptuous
domineering	arrogant, overbearing, controlling
deceitful	dishonest, deceptive, duplicitous
manipulative	devious, exploitative, calculating
insincere	superficial, slick, evasive
garrulous	glib, verbose, pretentious

ATTACHMENT	
detached	remote, distant, cold
uncommitted	unfaithful, undevoted, cold
unempathetic	uncompassionate, cruel, callous
uncaring	inconsiderate, thoughtless, neglectful
COGNITIVE	
suspicious	distrustful, guarded, hypervigilant
lacks concentration	distractible, inattentive, unfocused
intolerant	narrow-minded, bigoted, hypercritical
inflexible	stubborn, rigid, uncompromising
lacks planfulness	aimless, unsystematic, disorganized
BEHAVIORAL	
lacks perseverance	idle, undisciplined, unconscientious
unreliable	undependable, untrustworthy, irresponsible
reckless	rash, impetuous, risk-taking
restless	overactive, fidgety, energetic
disruptive	disobedient, unruly, unmanageable
aggressive	threatening, violent, bullying
Note: Adapted from Cooke et al., 2012, Figure 1 data, page 246.	

On Incremental Refinement vs. Transformative Change in Psychopathy Measurement

There have not been any revolutionary changes in how psychopathy or juvenile psychopathy is measured. When revisions occur, most instruments or versions constitute incremental enhancements rather than paradigm shifts. The Short Psychopathy Rating Scale (SPRS; Međedović, 2024) serves an as example. It is a new tool that is meant for adults. It uses established trait domains like deceitfulness, emotional coldness, and recklessness instead of establishing a completely new set of traits. This seems reasonable; however, the same issues discussed above remain. Its main contribution is that it is short, easy to use, and flexible enough for use by both experts and laypersons. Though not explicitly noted, one can imagine a future version aimed toward youth applications. Instruments specifically designed for youth, such as the Youth Psychopathic Traits Inventory (YPI) and its abbreviated version, the YPI-S (Andershed, Kerr, Stattin, & Levander, 2002), maintain the same foundational three-factor model (interpersonal, affective, behavioral) and have undergone refinement primarily through cross-cultural validation and invariance testing (e.g., Boonmann et al., 2020); Ebrahimi, Athar, Bakhshizadeh, Lavasani, & Andershed, 2022). Recent studies also continue to assess the YPI-S seeking to validate its factorial validity and reliability across linguistic and gender demographics. Hence, youth measures, and psychopathy instruments generally, largely grow by psychometric refinement, not full reconceptualization.

This orientation to measurement development has both positive and negative effects. The virtue in incremental development is that it maintains continuity with decades of research, allowing for direct comparisons across studies and promoting meta-analytic integration. It also helps make sure that advancements in measuring (youth) psychopathy, including shorter scales, improved readability, and cross-cultural invariance, are still based on established findings. The consequence of this conservatism, however, is that it may keep current problems going, such as relying on antisocial conduct as a core feature, depending on self-report or third-party judgments, and necessarily being sensitive to developmental complexity. In other words, the field is in danger of putting *old wine in new skins*, which would make things appear novel but still constrained by the same assumptions.

Another issue that surrounds the measures of psychopathy, which will be discussed in the next chapter, involves variants of psychopathy. It may be that multiple pathways lead to the same outcome (equifinality), and this justifies uniting all the observed primary and secondary "symptoms" for psychopathy under one conceptual umbrella. The rationale for doing this is linked to a need to appropriately identify individuals and to devise treatment. However, there are some issues with this as it may ultimately complicate efforts to devise treatments, a concern repeatedly echoed throughout this work.

CHAPTER 2 MAIN POINTS

❖ A generally agreed upon definition of psychopathy remains elusive.

❖ There are real concerns over the measures used to capture psychopathy and particularly juvenile psychopathy.

❖ Ways to operationalize the construct of psychopathy remain in question as long as the defining features of the disorder have not been consistently elucidated.

❖ Much of the concern with operationalizing psychopathy centers around using behavioral items to measure the construct.

❖ The research concerning developmental psychopathy is heterogeneous owning to the definition and operationalization problems.

❖ Using forensic samples may be problematic and add to the confusion surrounding the disorder.

❖ Scholars are attempting to move beyond the definition and measurement issues but this activity is emergent and does not reflect the breadth of psychopathy research.

❖ Labelling a youth as a psychopath, particularly in the current empirical environment, raises inherent concerns as many items included in measures are seen in normal adolescent development and or are argued to have criterion contamination.

CHAPTER 3

VARIANTS OF PSYCHOPATHY

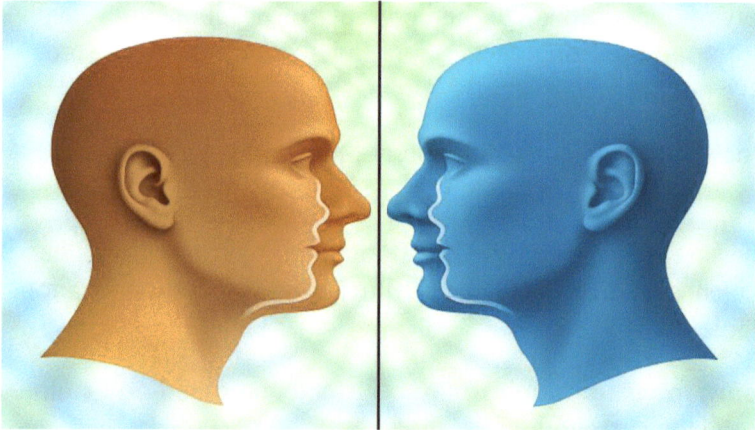

What is Variant Juvenile (Nascent) Psychopathy and

Why is it Important?

The identification of different manifestations and perhaps etiologies have led some to theorize that there are different types of psychopathy or variants. This is not to say that psychopathy should be thought of in terms of "type" based on prevailing symptomology, e.g., the impulsive type, the criminal type, etcetera though some have argued for such a scheme. Rather, distinctions might be useful if variants can be thought of in terms of differing etiologies that may lead to the label of psychopathy. The discussion now turns to how different pathways may result in a label of psychopath. This is crucially important because if the cause of one's psychopathy or psychopathic-like state is not identified, then (again) how can treatments be developed? Arguably, assuming all psychopaths, or those labelled as such, are the same is not advisable given the research.

Karpman's Primary and Secondary Psychopaths

Variations of psychopathy have been theorized that bear on the discussion of etiology or cause. Quite simply, establishing if multiple causes exist will tell us how different treatments may have to evolve to accommodate different needs and deficits.

Karpman (1941) is credited as the first to theorize about primary and secondary variants of psychopathy, which represent different causal pathways and manifestations of psychopathic-like states and traits. This delineation of psychopathy as primary or secondary clearly reflects Karpan's training as a medical doctor (specializing in psychiatry) as many medical ailments are understood based on whether they are defined as primary or secondary conditions. Appreciating contexts by these classifications helps with understanding processes, needs and treatments.

Very briefly, one can understand a primary condition as an essential or underlying condition and the secondary condition as "secondary to" some primary. For example, a broken bone would be considered a primary condition, with pain (or muscle wasting, etc.) "secondary to" the break. You would not treat the condition of pain without treating the primary condition, the break. In fact, treatment would require addressing or treating the break (primary condition), and this would be ulti-

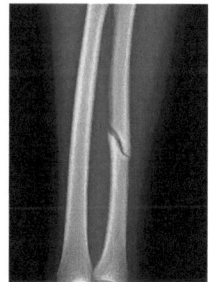

mately curative of the pain (secondary condition). In the context of disease states, a secondary disease would be caused by an earlier disease. Secondary can also be understood as "secondary to" some other factor. To illustrate further, while Type 1 diabetes would be considered a primary disease, the steroid prednisone can cause diabetes. Here, the prednisone-induced diabetes would be considered secondary diabetes. Karpman theorized about psychopathy in this way.

To Karpman, primary psychopathy is seemingly representative of those with idiopathic (or heritable) psychopathic traits, as discussed previously, and represents those having severe affective deficit (Karpman, 1941). The primary psychopath, to Karpamn, is the true psychopath. The term secondary psychopath represents individuals meeting some criteria for psychopathy, often measured by behaviors and differentially linked attributes, but were believed to result from unique environmental factors that led to the emergence of psychopathic characteristics. He criticized how these secondary individuals were thrown into the psychopathy catch-all basket, which severely compromised the ability to understand the condition.

Karpman believed secondary individuals were tantamount to psychopathic mimics or having a psychopathic façade, and the manifestation of the psychopathy or psychopathic-like tendencies was secondary to early disturbances, such as trauma and abuse, or manifestations of other psychiatric conditions. Here, for example, behavioral outbursts as a manifestation of what appeared to be psychopathy may be secondary to some maladaptation and or other psychiatric condition. Deal with the maladaptation or psychiatric circumstance (primary issue), and you will manage the psychopathic-like tendencies such as callousness or behavioral outbursts (secondary issue) that led to the psychopathy diagnosis.

According to Karpman:

Thus, so far as I can see, the understanding of the psychopathic personality, in spite of the efforts made to elicit it, still escapes us for the most part. It is a question whether the clinically described psychopathic personality exists. There is little doubt that many people become entangled with law and equally as many people, who while not directly involved with law, showed marked antisocial traits, but I see no justification for calling them psychopathic since a closer study of these cases would reveal them as belonging to other cardinal groups.

In order to bring some order out of this chaos and clear out the Augean stables, I have proposed a drastic division of all that is grouped under the heading of psychopathic personality, into two groups: I speak of one as symptomatic or secondary, and the other as primary or idiopathic... In the group of symptomatic, I include all those cases which beyond the symptoms given show on actual study that the psychopathic reaction, however severe it may appear on the surface, is traceable to some definite psychic influences that fall within the framework of other clinical types.... I would thus remove from the group of psychopathic personalities those psychopaths whose difficulties are traced to definite psychogenic factors and merely designate them according to the original diagnosis.

1948, p. 525-526

Of interest, Cleckley (1976, p. 239) remarks on Karpman:

In these studies [by Karpman] the very great egocentrici-

ty, the inability to form any important or binding attachment to another, the failure ever to realize and grasp the very meaning of responsibility, all features that I believe to be most essential, are emphasized by Karpman and made clear as seldom done in other literature on the psychopath.

Some may argue that Karpman's observations are dated and that we have come much further since then. One only needs to examine the landscape of research on the topic to realize quite readily that we are not that far along. However, research exploring delineations in the development of psychopathy is still emerging (for discussion see Vaughn, Edens, Howard, & Smith, 2009). While studies on the two distinct etiological pathways are scarce, scholars have observed characteristically different types of psychopathy paralleling this notion of primary and secondary psychopathy in adults (e.g., Skeem, Johansson, Andershed, Kerr, & Louden, 2007) and adolescents (Vaughn et al., 2009). With respect to youth, research examining variant juvenile offenders has isolated a group having lower levels of psychological distress, which is in concert with the theorized primary type as having low affect (Vaughn et al., 2009). Those mirroring the secondary variant were more likely to have a history of trauma, be diagnosed with attention-deficit hyperactivity disorder, present with higher delinquency and drug use, and were also more likely to suffer from higher affective distress and emotional turmoil; While these findings are theoretically consistent with the secondary variant as being more prone to anxiety, reactance, hostility, and impulsivity, as well as being influenced by environmental factors (Vaughn et al., 2009, p. 182), these co-occurring characteristics

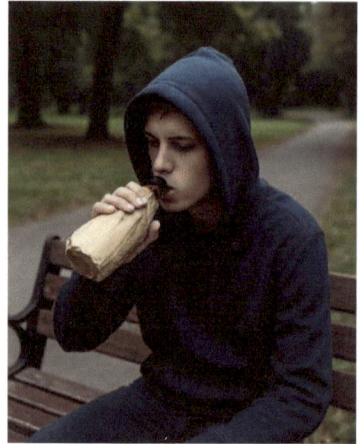

also seem to detract from clarity and may frustrate attempts to define and understand psychopathy. Indeed, we may still be throwing all psychopathic-like youth into the same catch-all basket. Whether this ultimately serves the interest of these youth is in question.

Measuring Variants

The measurement of secondary psychopathy is entering a new phase. Recent work has begun to move beyond the traditional *CU + anxiety* shorthand and toward approaches that capture the distinct vulnerabilities of the secondary variant. Though there are many examples, only a few are covered here. For example, Coelho et al. (2025) demonstrate that secondary psychopathy is marked not by fearlessness but by a broader, socially oriented fear profile, while Oba et al. (2024) use network modeling to show how secondary traits cluster with anxiety, ADHD, and autistic communication difficulties. Flexon & Encalada (2021) add a developmental lens, tracing how early adversity and disrupted attachments predict the emergence of secondary-like traits over time. A recent narrative review by Almas & Lordos (2025) underscores the need for new measurement strategies, though largely reiterating earlier theoretical treatments, and highlights the potential of qualitative perspectives to enrich this discussion. Together, these advances point toward more valid, multidimensional approaches to capturing secondary psychopathy in both research and applied contexts.

A persistent challenge in psychopathy research is how to measure the proposed variants in a way that captures their distinct qualities. Most of the existing instruments were built with the *primary* type in mind, and they tend to focus on callous–unemotional traits or interpersonal coldness. As a result, the *secondary* variant is often assessed indirectly, through markers such as impulsivity, aggression, or comorbid disorders, rather than by instruments designed to capture its defining features.

The Levenson Self-Report Psychopathy Scale (LSRP) remains the most commonly used tool to distinguish between primary and secondary psychopathy, especially in community samples (Levenson, Kiehl, & Fitzpatrick, 1995). Its two-factor model is consistent with Karpman's framework, but the secondary dimension largely reflects impulsivity and behavioral instability rather than the anxiety, trauma, and emotional dysregulation theorized to underlie this pathway. The Psychopathic Personality Inventory (PPI) provides some coverage of secondary traits through its "Self-Centered Impulsivity" scale (Lilienfeld & Andrews, 1996), yet this was not the intent of the instrument's design.

Recent research has started to fill these gaps. Coelho et al. (2025) combined the LSRP with a comprehensive fear survey and found that secondary psychopathy is not characterized by fearlessness but by a *broader and more typical profile of fears*, such as humiliation and abandonment. In contrast, individuals high in primary psychopathy endorsed far fewer and less conventional fears. This suggests that the problem is not the absence of fear in the secondary group but the presence of excessive and socially oriented fears.

Equally important is the narrative review by Almas & Lordos (2025), which offers a contemporary framework for understanding secondary psychopathy. They argue that existing measures have been biased toward the heritable, affective-deficit profile of primary psychopathy, leaving the secondary type underrepresented. Their review calls for new assessment strategies that explicitly integrate trauma history, anxiety sensitivity, and emotional dysregulation, ideally using multiple methods, e.g., self-report, informant ratings, and behavioral observation, to capture the complexity of this variant.

Adding to this perspective, Oba et al. (2024) used network analysis to map psychopathy alongside other traits. They found that secondary psychopathy connects closely with ADHD symptoms, autistic communication traits, and trait anxiety. This approach highlights the extent to which secondary psychopathy overlaps with other vulnerabilities and suggests that network methods may provide a more accurate picture than traditional factor models.

Together, these studies signal a shift in how secondary psychopathy is conceptualized and measured. Rather than treating it as a residual category, recent work highlights its distinctive emotional and developmental profile. Moving forward, instruments that account for fear content, trauma, and co-occurring vulnerabilities are likely to provide more valid and clinically useful assessments of the secondary variant.

Variants and Anti-Sociality

Findings on the link between psychopathy variants and violence have often been mixed, but newer approaches to measurement are beginning to clarify the picture. Secondary psychopathy, traditionally identified by CU traits in combination with anxiety as noted, has emerged as the variant most consistently linked with reactive aggression (or violence generally) when fear, trauma, and impulsivity are measured directly. By contrast, the primary variant shows a weaker and less consistent connection to violent behavior, particularly in community samples. Specifically, research is emerging that suggests that the secondary variant is at greater risk for engaging in violence among noninstitutionalized samples (Fanti et al., 2013; Flexon, 2015, 2016). Some of these findings reveal no association between the primary type and violent behavior at all, while the secondary type is significantly associated with violence (Flexon, 2015, 2016).

If the primary variant in youth can be conceived of as having a callous–unemotional interpersonal style alone, and the secondary variant is attached to multiple vulnerabilities (e.g., impulsivity), this finding is in concert with Camp, Skeem, Barchard, Lilienfeld, and Poythress (2013, p. 2), who note that "there is little evidence that those with high Hare's Psychopathy Checklist Revised (PCL-R) scores [for psychopathy] are at risk for committing violence chiefly because they are cold-hearted, callous, or emotionally detached." In fact, these researchers caution against making overly broad characterizations about psychopathy and violence, observing that it is largely Factor 2, the Social Deviance scale of the PCL-R (Hare, 1991), that better predicts violence.

This second factor, meant to measure unstable and antisocial lifestyle, is manifested by antagonism, anger, and impulsivity (Camp, Skeem, Barchard, Lilienfeld, & Poythress, 2013). Impulsivity is particularly implicated in violence and general delinquency (de Ridder, Lensvelt-Mulders, Finkenauer, Stok, & Baumeister, 2012; Flexon & Meldrum, 2013; Pratt & Cullen, 2000), apart from being united with Hare's conceptualization of psychopathy. Impulsivity or low self-control has long been associated with antisociality, as well as being linked with similar causal forces as the secondary variant. Ineffective or problematic parenting, for instance, has been shown to precipitate the emergence of troubling attributes and the resulting antisocial behaviors. This recognition is consistent with findings disaggregating youth by variant type, which reveal that primary callous–unemotional youth in a national sample were less likely to engage in violence compared to others in the sample (Flexon, 2015).

Traditionally, secondary psychopathy has often been identified by combining CU traits with an anxiety scale, and it is this very blend of callousness and reactivity that appears most predictive of violence

(Skeem et al., 2003; Vaughn et al., 2009). Flexon & Encalada (2021) deepen this picture by showing how contextual forces such as poverty, parenting, and attachment insecurity act as antecedents to secondary-like traits, providing the developmental roots of the same vulnerabilities that increase violence risk.

At the same time, some research has suggested that primary youth may be more aggressive than lower-risk youth in certain community samples (Fanti et al., 2013), leading to mixed findings concerning the primary variant and antisocial behavior among the non-incarcerated. Such conflicts in the literature often stem from how psychopathy is measured. For instance, Fanti, Demetriou, and Kimonis (2013) treated conduct problems as part of the defining traits of psychopathic-like variants and found an association between primary psychopathic-like youth and aggression. By contrast, Flexon (2015, 2016) did not incorporate conduct problems in defining variants and did not find an association between primary youth and violence. Including antisocial behavior in the measurement scheme risks tautology: the same behavior is used both to define the construct and to predict related outcomes.

As discussed earlier, these inconsistencies point to measurement heterogeneity as one of the most pressing challenges for research in this area. Recent work, however, has begun to clarify why violence is more consistently associated with the secondary variant. Coelho et al. (2025) showed that socially oriented fears (e.g., humiliation, abandonment) make reactivity and aggression more likely. Almas & Lordos (2025), while largely reiterating earlier theoretical frameworks, emphasize that current measures privilege primary features and miss the vulnerabilities central to the secondary type. Oba et al. (2024) further demonstrated that secondary psychopathy clusters with impulsivity, anxiety, and neurodevelopmental traits, providing plausible pathways to aggression.

In short, inconsistencies in findings on aggression may reflect measurement artifacts rather than true theoretical contradictions. When instruments incorporate impulsivity, trauma, and fear content, the secondary variant consistently emerges as the group most vulnerable to reactive violence and entanglement in the justice system. The following figure (Figure 3.1) very simply illustrates the theoretical paths by variant to aggressive/violent behavior.

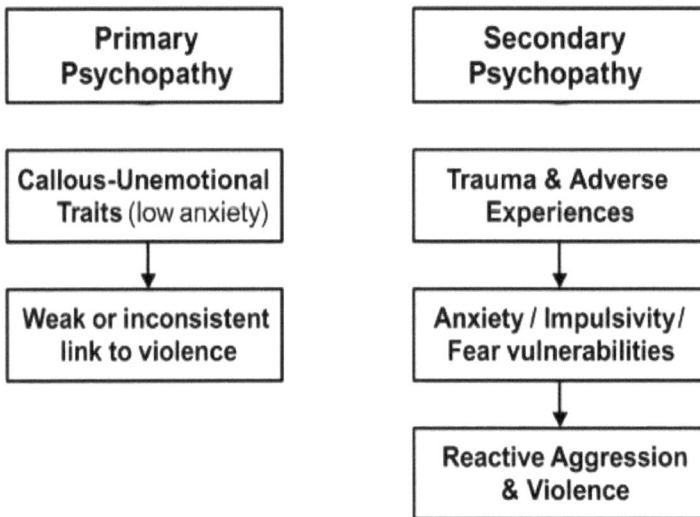

Note: For Secondary Psychopathy, there is a more consistent link when measured with multidimensional tools (fear, trauma, impulsivity).

Figure 3.1

In practicality, how does this move the bar toward understanding psychopathy and devising successful treatment? It seems reasonable to conclude that certain circumstances may create or manifest psychopathic features in an individual. The result may look similar to the idiopathic or genetically predisposed type that has no choice about having particular affect, for instance. Someone born a certain way compared to someone created through serious developmental trauma, abuse or other disturbances may crucially end up at the same place. This has obvious implications and does matter for understanding and treatment. It is important to note that since some have connected the primary variant specifically with the affective deficits (Factor 1, affective facet) of psychopathy and less impulsivity (Factor 2, lifestyle facet) than secondary psychopaths (Skeem et al., 2003, p. 529), it may be the secondary variant's connection to impulsivity that may be driving part of the association between psychopathy generally and aggression. This is difficult to sort through, however, as much research does not disaggregate psychopathy by variant type. Thus, examining the interplay between abuse, parenting, impulsivity, and outcomes by variant type is important, but more research is clearly needed before drawing definitive conclusions.

To illustrate this connection with aggressive behavior by variant type, Table 3.1 displays a value based measure of self-reported violent acts reported by youth deemed non-psychopathic, and primary and secondary psychopathic-like in a general sample. Data from the NICHD's SECCYD were used to construct the table. It is important to note upfront that statistical significance tests were not conducted with the table as it was produced for illustrative purposes and to avoid adding technical jargon (i.e., < 5 count per cell, etcetera). For those interested, statistical tests and equations can be found in prior work demonstrating the relationships (i.e., Flexon, 2015, 2016).

For the violence measure reported in Table 3.1, which was adapted from Conger and Elder (1994), items included whether the youth had taken part in a gang fight, attacked someone, been in a fight between kids, used a weapon to threaten someone, stolen something with the use of a weapon, threatened to attack someone with a weapon, beat someone without a weapon, beat someone with a weapon, and hurt an animal on purpose. The created violence scale ranged from 0 through 8 and is consistent with prior research (see Flexon, 2016). Primary youth in this table include only those demonstrating affective deficits, while secondary youth have the affective deficits along with anxiety, which is often used to delineate the two variant types. Conduct problems were not included as one of the features identifying the disorder.

Table 3.1 Violent * Psychopathy Group Summary Tabulation					
		Psychopathy Group			
Violence Value		Non-Psychopath	Primary	Secondary	N
0	Count	625	38	87	750
	% within	85.0	86.4	62.6	81.7
1	Count	73	3	25	101
	% within	9.9	6.8	18.0	11.0
2	Count	28	1	8	37
	% within	3.8	2.3	5.8	4.0
3	Count	3	1	10	14
	% within	0.4	2.3	7.2	1.5
4	Count	3	0	5	8
	% within	0.4	0.0	3.6	0.9
5	Count	1	1	1	3
	% within	0.1	2.3	0.7	0.3
6	Count	1	0	2	3
	% within	0.1	0.0	1.4	0.3
7	Count	0	0	1	1
	% within	0.0	0.0	0.7	0.1
8	Count	1	0	0	1
	% within	0.1	0.0	0.0	0.1
Total	Count	735	44	139	918
	% within	100.0	100.0	100.0	100.0

From the table, secondary psychopaths show stronger tendencies toward violence compared to the other two groups in this sample (Flexon, 2015, 2016). This finding is important because it suggests that *other features beyond callous–unemotional traits* are driving the connection to aggressive and violent behavior, particularly in general populations. Recent research strengthens this point. When secondary psychopathy is measured with tools that capture fear content, trauma, and impulsivity, for example, it more reliably predicts violence risk (Almas & Lordos, 2025; Coelho et al., 2025; Oba et al., 2024). These studies demonstrate that it is not fearlessness or emotional detachment alone that explains aggression, but the co-occurrence of vulnerabilities, including heightened anxiety, dysregulation, and social fears, that characterize the secondary variant.

By contrast, null or mixed findings for primary youth may partly stem from instruments that emphasize CU traits while underrepresenting the vulnerabilities most relevant to aggression. In this way, the numbers from Table 3.1 also align with research showing that Factor 2 of the PCL-R (reflecting impulsivity and unstable lifestyle) better predicts aggressive behavior than the affective dimension of Factor 1, even amidst the measurement inconsistencies discussed earlier. The implication is that violence among youth high in psychopathic traits is less about coldness per se' and more about the cluster of co-occurring traits, impulsivity, fear, trauma-linked anxiety, that amplify risk. This reframes the question: is it callousness on its own that creates the pathway to violence, or is it these layered vulnerabilities, attached to the secondary profile, that better explain why certain youth with psy

It is also worth noting that violent acts are a rare entity, which is demonstrated with the table. For those engaging in more violent acts, there is arguably a higher probability of getting caught up in the criminal justice system. This perhaps makes secondary youth (and adults) more represented in forensic samples used to define and inform ideas about psychopathy. As a result of this, the image of psychopathy may be contaminated by other co-occurring conditions or tendencies. This was the concern expressed by Karpman.

Variants and Etiological Pathways

Understanding the origins of psychopathy requires distinguishing between inherited dispositions and environmentally acquired adaptations. While primary psychopathy is often linked to idiopathic or genetic traits, secondary psychopathy has increasingly been traced to developmental adversities such as trauma, neglect, and disrupted attachment. Recent longitudinal studies, alongside classic theoretical accounts, are helping to clarify how these different etiological pathways produce outwardly similar but causally distinct psychopathic profiles.

Porter (1996, p. 180) argued that "two distinct etiological pathways, one primarily congenital and one primarily environmental, can culminate phenotypically as a psychopathic personality." Along with this recognition, strong empirical evidence exists that all psychopaths are not created equal. This is important (again) because in order to address treatment better understanding of the pathways toward psychopathy is needed. For example, in the case of those born with reduced or absent affective traits, genetic variation is potentially causative and a response might be one to acquaint and teach the individual, even in the abstract, what such emotive capacity is and means toward informing socially appropriate behavior. If someone makes it to psychopathy as a result of emotional blunting or numbing as a consequence of prior abuse, trauma or neglect in childhood or adolescence, the treatment options would likely be quite different. This difference may be viewed along a continuum of habilitation through to rehabilitation.

Porter's (1996) isolation of causal pathways recognizes that early traumas may influence the emergence of psychopathy, which is characteristic of Karpman's secondary psychopath. Porter notes that because the cause may be rooted in abuse, trauma, or neglect that emergent (secondary) psychopaths may be learning to effectively dissociate by turning off their emotions as a coping mechanism. He further argues that this secondary form of psychopathy should be treated as "a distinctive dissociative disorder based on this detachment of emotion and cognition/ behavior" (Porter, 1996, p. 179).

Concerning the secondary variant, Kerig et al. (2012) also has suggested that emotional numbing is a mechanism used by youth to reconcile abuses and trauma. This numbing arguably contributes to an *acquired callousness* in youth, and this callousness, in turn, promotes anti-social behaviors. In that way, the acquired callousness as observed in some youth mirrors Karpman's description concerning the etiology of the secondary variant. For example, Kerig et al.'s (2012) work with youth from detention centers indicates that the general numbing of emotions mediated the association between trauma exposure (in the presence of betrayal) and CU traits. This finding offers an important distinction among variants as many scholars and clinicians lament that psychopathy is immutable and untreatable. If the secondary variant acquires their callous traits as a dissociative adaptation, then there is hope for intervention and treatment (see Skeem et al., 2003), particularly because secondary variants arguably have the capacity to experience normal affect. Such findings point to the necessity of understanding the differences and similarities between variants of youth scoring high on CU traits.

Research also indicates that primary youth who experience abuse by their mothers are at risk for abhorrent behaviors (Kimonis et al., 2013). The finding suggests that the volatile behavior represents a maladaptive response among the primary variant as seen with the secondary variant. Since though (and yet to be validated), abuse and trauma from the parents help shape the secondary variants CU traits and primary variants are arguably born with them, there may be 1) a multiplicative effect on behavior from having CU traits alongside abuse or neglect, and/or 2) abuse or neglect is creating a disruption in behavior irrespective of whether CU traits are innately present since is it a robust predictor of a range of youth behaviors and both variants may simply learn parental anti-social tactics that have been successful toward some end (e.g., cycle of violence, intergenerational transmissions), and or 3) CU traits partially moderates the relationship between parental abuse or neglect and aggression.

Flexon & Encalada (2021) extend this line of evidence by tracing how contextual forces such as poverty, lower maternal education, authoritarian parenting, and insecure attachment predict the emergence of secondary-like psychopathy in adolescence. Their findings underscore that environmental adversity and relational disruption operate as antecedents in a longitudinal framework, placing secondary psychopathy firmly within a developmental-etiological framework rather than one defined solely by personality traits.

It should also be noted that there still is some disagreement concerning whether aggregating psychopathy is meaningful as much research looking at youth psychopathy examines it as a unified concept or whether treating all psychopaths the same in research and practice lends to more confusion. This concern was briefly noted. Sentiments expressing the opposite also seem apparent. In other words, if somebody has psychopathy, does it matter if they are one variant or another? Does it mean that, essentially, if your psychopathic, once you get there that there is no reason to extend inquiry?

The research seems to be pointing toward this notion of variants (see also Hare, 2016). Arguably, it is also important because the notion that psychopathy is immutable is debatable and if a psychopathic-like youth got there by means of early trauma or abuse, but they have the capacities of an arguably "normal" person, then rehabilitation or habilitation is possible. Here, if somebody's psychopathic-like because they are dissociative and there was a failure to be properly socialized as a result of the same occurrences, that is poor, neglectful or abusive parenting, then treatment is not only meaningful but a duty. In parallel, if someone got to psychopathy because of idiopathic or genetic traits, then there is a duty to these youths to manage the attributes that may lend to unhealthy or anti-social outcomes. If it is found that these cannot be altered, then other conversations need to be had and alternative strategies developed. Hence, unpacking the heterogeneous contours of psychopathy is paramount for understanding and will inform everything that then flows from that point.

Table 3.2 presents a theoretical map for how psychopathy may emerge through two different pathways. While epigenetic influences are operating throughout (discussed later in Chapter 6), it capitalizes on the ideas that primary psychopathy is associated with heritable temperamental and neurobiological differences, whereas secondary psychopathy reflects the epigenetic embedding of early trauma and adverse childhood experiences. Mapping these distinct, though theoretical, trajectories highlights potential intervention points for prevention and treatment, which are discussed in the next chapter.

Table 3.2 Two Distinct Pathways to Psychopathy	
PATHWAY TO PRIMARY PSYCHOPATHY	**PATHWAY TO SECONDARY PSYCHOPATHY**
1. Genetic and Temperamental Predispositions	**1. Adverse Childhood Experiences (ACEs)**
Strong heritability for low fear reactivity, low anxiety, and blunted emotional responsiveness. Fearlessness and reward dominance often visible in early childhood.	Abuse, neglect, household dysfunction, and exposure to violence create *chronic toxic stress* during sensitive developmental periods.

2. Neurobiological Differences (Present Early)	2. Chronic Stress Response Activation
Reduced amygdala responsiveness to threat/distress cues. Structural and functional differences in prefrontal and paralimbic regions. Altered connectivity between emotional and decision-making brain networks.	Overactive hypothalamic–pituitary–adrenal (HPA) axis → sustained cortisol release and inflammatory signaling.
3. Epigenetic Influences	3. Epigenetic Modifications
(Predisposition Shaping) Gene expression patterns reinforce low emotional reactivity and high sensation-seeking. Environment plays a smaller causal role than in secondary psychopathy but can magnify traits in permissive or anti-social contexts.	DNA methylation and histone modification in genes linked to stress regulation, emotion, and aggression. Changes alter gene expression without changing DNA sequence.
4. Behavioral Manifestations	4. Neurobiological Disruption
Callous–unemotional traits, lack of empathy or guilt, calculated aggression, manipulativeness, and emotional detachment.	Impaired prefrontal cortex development. Altered amygdala–prefrontal connectivity. Heightened threat sensitivity or emotional dysregulation.

5. Potential Intervention Points	5. Behavioral Manifestations
Early identification of CU traits. Structured, consistent environments rewarding prosocial behavior. Explore neurocognitive and future epigenetic interventions.	Secondary psychopathy traits: impulsivity, aggression, emotional volatility, and antisocial behavior as trauma adaptation.
	6. Potential Intervention Points
	Prevention: reduce ACE exposure. Trauma-informed therapy. Future epigenetic therapies to reverse maladaptive gene expression patterns.

CHAPTER 3 MAIN POINTS

❖ Psychopathy may be better understood as being either primary or secondary in character and origin.

❖ Treating all psychopaths or those being in a psychopathic-like state as the same is not advisable given the current state of research.

❖ Recognizing that psychopathy variants display different vulnerabilities may lend to better treatments.

❖ Karpman's theory that primary psychopaths were idiopathic and secondary psychopaths were made through environment is a contention that some research seems to support.

❖ Secondary variants seem to be much more inclined to commit acts of violence and criminal acts, as well as being attached to more vulnerabilities than the primary variant.

❖ Anxiety is often used to delineate primary and secondary variants, whereas primary variants lack anxiety, which is more in line with original conceptions of psychopathy, and the secondary presents with anxiety.

❖ Conceptual and measurement issues continue to aggravate attempts to understand variants of psychopathy.

❖ New research (e.g., Coelho et al., 2025; Flexon & Encalda, 2020; Oba et al., 2024) highlights that inconsistencies in aggression findings often stem from measurement heterogeneity. When assessed with multidimensional tools, secondary psychopathy consistently emerges as more strongly linked to reactive aggression.

CHAPTER 4

TREATMENT STRATEGIES

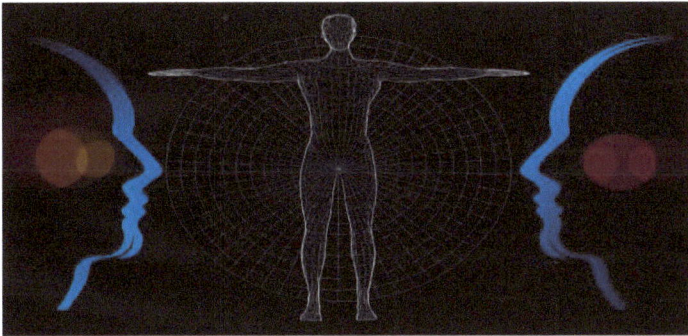

Is Treatment Possible?

While it remains unclear to what extent research findings will continue to elucidate similarities and differences in the concept of child psychopathy, scientific findings, as they currently stand, may be encouraging for the treatment of psychopathy in children and adolescents. That is, research results such as the overlap with internalizing disorders and potentially less stability may be indicative of better amenability (Citations Omitted). This is because such differences (e.g., co-existing anxiety) may give researchers more leads in understanding the potential causal factors linked to psychopathy (Citation Omitted). However, these are, admittedly, mostly suppositions at this point, which leads to the question of what do we really know about the treatment of psychopathy?

Salekin, Worley, & Grimes, 2010, p. 240

It is important to note upfront that practitioners employ various assessment tools to screen youth for intervention and treatment needs. Screening for psychopathic traits has become much more common for institutional intake, as well as for informing the courts of future of- fending risk. So, there are distinctions that can be drawn with respect to the purpose of the assessment: mental health considerations; duty of care/child protection; prediction of future dangerousness; etcetera. For the purposes here, we will treat assessment (and intervention) as though these tools are used for informing need for treatment. While the following chapter, Chapter 5, focuses on legal aspects related to as- sessing psychopathy in youth for use by the courts and will touch upon risk assessment, similar issues are addressed here because the presence of problem behavior indicates a condition that interferes with healthy functioning and needs treatment. With that in mind, it's important to mention upfront that the conversation below will necessarily inter- twine findings addressing youth with CU traits alone and that examin- ing youth with CU traits and adjoining externalizing behaviors (con- duct problems).

Intervention Access Points

Though some have cautioned against the clinical and nonclinical use of the term psychopathy, particularly in reference to youth, there is reason to include measures for CU traits (and low self-control) at the earliest point of access to troubled youth for intervention and treatment purposes. Contrary to accepted sentiment that psychopathy, or other inherent personality difficulties, is resistant to treatment, some have cautioned against making such dividing lines regarding treatability (Salekin, 2002; Salekin, Worley, & Grimes, 2010). It also appears that discerning among psychopathic type, i.e., primary or secondary, would be highly advisable when seeking out treatment strategies. As noted earlier, this is often done by isolating the absence (Primary type) or presence (Secondary type) of anxiety. However, on this point, little work has been done, but there has been movement more generally on trying to isolate treatment protocols for psychopathy, which have included youth. It should also be mentioned that treatment response may also differ by psychopathic variant (see Comment Box: Variant-Specific Treatment Considerations). In order to properly identify appropriate strategies, it is paramount to discuss nascent psychopathy within a broader landscape of literature on the causes of juvenile crime. There is a plethora of perspectives on this front in the criminological literature; however, the discussion here will be limited to that related to early trauma.

The Role of Adverse Childhood Experiences (ACEs)

It is readily accepted that early trauma is influential in the path toward aggressive behavior. In fact, the research is ubiquitous. In like way, this is also the case with psychopathic-like youth (see e.g., Flexon & Encalada, 2020; Kimonis, Cross, Howard, & Donoghue, 2013, on the link between parenting, maltreatment, and CU traits among juvenile offenders). This can be thought of through another lens of well-established research. Adverse Childhood Experiences, or ACEs, provide a systematic framework for understanding this trauma. ACEs refer to potentially traumatic events before the age of 18, such as physical abuse, neglect, exposure to domestic violence, parental substance misuse, or even the incarceration of a caregiver. The original ACE study, conducted by the CDC and Kaiser Permanente, documented a strong graded relationship between the number of adverse experiences and a wide range of mental health, behavioral, and health outcomes in adulthood (see Felitti et al., 1998, the foundational ACE study). Within this work, a threshold effect is often noted where individuals with four or more ACEs are substantially more likely to experience severe outcomes, including substance dependence, suicidality, and risky behaviors. More recent research shows that youth offenders are disproportionately affected by ACEs, with some studies suggesting that nearly 90% of incarcerated youth report at least one ACE, and many reporting four or more (see Astridge, Li, McDermott, & Longhitano, 2023 for a systematic review of prevalence and recidivism and Gray, Smithson, & Jump, 2021 on ACEs and serious youth violence).

Importantly, ACEs are not only linked to later-life health problems but also to aggression, poor impulse control, and difficulty with authority, all traits often found among youth with psychopathic-like characteristics. Neurodevelopmental research has clarified that chronic trauma alters brain development by keeping the stress-response system in a heightened state of activation, thereby disrupting areas of the brain tied to emotional regulation, decision-making, and risk assessment. For youth who later present with secondary psychopathy, this pattern of developmental adversity and maladaptive adaptation is particularly salient. In such cases, violent or impulsive responses can be understood as survival-driven adaptations rather than static traits (see Jackson, Jones, Semenza, & Testa, 2023 for relevant findings on mediators linking ACEs in middle childhood to adolescent delinquency).

Framing secondary psychopathy within the ACEs literature highlights an important treatment implication. That is, these youth may not be *hardwired* toward callousness in the same way that primary variants are hypothesized to be. Rather, their psychopathic-like presentation may reflect an adaptation to persistent adversity. This argument rests in the same orientation as theorists proposing that early trauma creates a dissociative adaptation in youth. Such an understanding opens space for trauma-informed approaches to intervention. Early intervention in the form of school-based trauma programs, family support services, mentorship, and accessible community mental health care can interrupt cycles of externalizing behavior and reduce the risk of entrenched psychopathic states. Treatment strategies that incorporate trauma-informed care, by recognizing *what happened to the child* instead of focusing solely on *what is wrong with the child*, are especially critical in addressing the secondary variant (see also Salekin, 2017).

The bottom line, ACEs research strengthens the argument that interventions should not only target the child but also the family and broader social environment. This is not a new idea. There are, in fact, *criminogenic* environments, and this is long recognized. Given this, preventing and treating trauma at early stages is crucial to altering the developmental trajectory toward aggression, delinquency, and psychopathic-like behavior.

Since the secondary variant is most implicated with co-morbid conditions and various forms of aggression, there is room for optimism. The secondary variant is considered to be more amenable to traditional treatment methods (Skeem et al., 2003), as well as being more responsive to external modalities to alter behavior (Kosson & Newman, 1995). Underscoring this view is a belief that secondary psychopaths are created through circumstance rather than being born with affective deficits, though this point remains debated. It may be that, given the evidence of mutability, secondary types may reflect those being in a psychopathic state, rather than having psychopathic traits. While this is an empirical question and in the absence of research clarifying this point, there is still need. Intervention should thus aim to interrupt the processes that arguably evoke secondary psychopathy and externalizing behaviors. Such processes were discussed in a previous chapter and are tied to the next point.

The family environment and in particular the behavior of parents is consistently implicated in the adaptation patterns and behavior of children and adolescents. It may be that similar stresses on youth from inept and even abusive parenting result in the emergence of several key criminological correlates, including the (arguably) secondary variant, impulsivity (Flexon, 2015, 2016), vulnerability to peers, may explain whom youth affiliate with (delinquent peers), as well as give clues to this variant's anxiety. Given this is the case, a central point of intervention is with the family/parents, which is consistent with theory. For instance, Karpman (1941, 1948) explicitly states that environmental stresses, such as parental abuse, evoke secondary psychopathy, and Gottfredson and Hirschi (1990) place parenting in eminence in creating youth with low self-control (impulsivity), which, to them, is the cause of crime and all analogous behaviors. The quality of parenting, then, may influence child/adolescent characteristics in a way that interferes with a youth having a healthy interface with their social environment. This would include making them more vulnerable to unhealthy affective states and externalizing behaviors, such as engaging in aggressive behavior (e.g., Kerig et al., 2012).

In sum, intervention aimed at the quality of the parent (or caregiver)–youth relationship prior to and in adolescence is likely key to influencing affective states and externalizing behaviors in youth. On this point, many covariates of problem youth behavior (except perhaps for the primary-like variant and even that is debatable) are subject to the behavior and actions of the parents, apart from the individual vulnerabilities of the adolescent (i.e., how the child/adolescent perceives and responds to the parent's actions; Beaver, Hartman, & Belsky, 2015). Further, findings from studies clearly indicate that the secondary-like variant is more likely to be associated with various vulnerabilities in addition to aggression irrespective of the motivation than the primary-like variant among the noninstitutionalized.

The above leads to the conclusion that for particular youth, something more than having CU traits is driving externalizing behaviors (see Salekin, 2017). It may be that the additional qualities needed are created by similar processes (i.e., parental neglect, abuse, hostility) that may culminate in the creation of multiple risk factors (e.g., callousness, unemotional interpersonal style, anxiety, and impulsivity). The picture is less clear concerning the primary-like variant though research already discussed has implicated parenting practices with externalizing behaviors for these primary youths. As such, risk assessment should be particularly mindful of evaluating the parent (caregiver)–youth relationship as being differentially implicated in the development of psychopathic-like states, as well as with the development of other known correlates of externalizing behavior. More on this point and additional risk factors are discussed in the following section and chapters.

Risk-Need-Responsivity (RNR) Principled Approach:

Coordinating Treatment

The risk-need-responsivity (RNR) approach, in this context, focuses on lowering risks associated with externalizing behaviors and criminogenic outcomes. Mitchell, Wormith, and Tafrate (2016) do a nice job of reviewing RNR and present a succinct description of the approach, which is a strategy readily used by professionals dealing with other types of clients. This is not a treatment per se, but rather a strategy to coordinate needs and services to lower externalizing behaviors.

Briefly, the *risk* component of RNR equivocates practitioner's efforts with the risk of offending (or with anti-social behaviors). Here, practitioners and or clinicians should utilize as many resources as needed to match the risk of externalizing behaviors. The *need* prong correlates treatment and intervention to the targeted criminogenic needs or risk factors of the individual. *Responsivity* (either general or specific) focuses on the use of behavioral and cognitive-behavioral approaches to lower risks of anti-social behaviors.

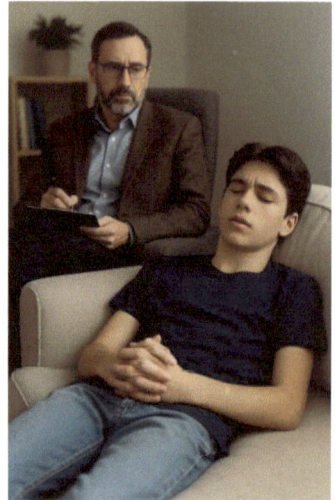

Specific approaches should be tailored to the individual characteristics of the offender or client. These approaches are used across different groups of institutionalized populations and are not new as already noted, and evaluations using the principles among psychopathic populations have been attempted (for review see White, Olver, & Lilienfeld, 2016). This research suggests that, "the criminogenic needs of psychopathic offenders are not different than those of non-psychopathic individuals; they tend to be more severe and probably larger in number" (White et al., 2016, p. 158). Since we are not exclusively dealing with criminality but with externalizing behaviors generally, tailoring approaches through RNR also is promising when it comes to dealing with different types of psychopathic youth and ties neatly with the approaches to be discussed.

United with this approach, there has been a reasonable amount of work among scholars in concert with the Office of Juvenile Justice and Delinquency Prevention (OJJDP) examining the risk factors associated with poor behavioral outcomes in youth, e.g., at-risk youth; serious, violent, and chronic (SVC) behavior. In addition to the family environment already discussed, the OJJDP offers a number of resources elaborating upon the known risk factors for problem behavior that could be used to inform the RNR approach. Although not expressly concerning psychopathic youth, given the above recognition concerning the increased needs of psychopathic individuals, it is possible that some of the strategies and programs identified by the OJJDP may work to ameliorate problems for CU youth. They have devoted significant resources examining what works, might work and what does not, which is available in an online model programs guide (see https://ojjdp.ojp.gov/model-programs-guide/home). In addition to these resources, there are real efforts among scholars and clinicians to develop strategies designed specifically for psychopathic-like youth.

Treatment Strategies for Psychopathic-Like Youth

As already touched upon, there is disagreement among scholars concerning whether psychopathy is amendable to treatment and whether initiating treatment has the potential to make the disorder worse (for discussion see

Salekin et al., 2010). Irrespective of these views, treatment should be attempted for several reasons. First, though seemingly contrary at first blush, given the contention surrounding the definition of psychopathy to the point that some argue that the condition doesn't even exist or

that if the PCL isn't being used then the research regarding treatment is arguably inferior (Harris & Rice, 2006), something has brought the youth to the attention of their parents, teachers or others that has elicited evaluation and a diagnosis akin to emerging psychopathy. Attempts to sort through the associated deficits or characteristics are therefore warranted as are attempts to help mitigate need and risk to and from the youth. Additionally, given there are problems with isolating psychopathy among youth, treatment may give rise to a more accurate diagnosis if some differential condition underlies the youth's difficulties. For example, the secondary psychopath, which is often delineated by the presence of anxiety, may not be purely psychopathic but rather resembles the psychopath (while this point may be quite controversial to some). Arguments aside, if anxiety can be used as a differential feature to some other primary condition, treatment may help to refine and clarify diagnosis and treatment needs.

Finally, scholars and clinicians are making attempts to treat psychopathy using already established methods with promising results. This suggests that efforts should continue despite the fatalistic stance that has plagued sentiments concerning psychopathy and treatability. The work of Salekin and colleagues (2010) crystalizes this point. In their review of programs involving the treatment of adults and youth having psychopathic traits, several studies showed promise, particularly those aimed at youth. More specifically, six of the eight studies dealing with youth showed that psychotherapy was either beneficial or at least psychopathic youth did no worse than non-psychopathic youth, suggesting that progress can be made or has potential to make a difference (p. 255). Interestingly, none of the programs were designed to specifically deal with youth diagnosed with psychopathy.

The authors recognized the concerns that certain psychopathic characteristics may inhibit treatment, but lamented that these features need not preclude treatment, but rather become a part of the treatment plan. For example, some have noted that psychopaths may be resistant to therapy and attempt manipulations to circumvent treatment. However, as scholars have noted, a number of patients with varied disorders present in a similar way to therapy (e.g., addiction). This has not stymied attempts at treatment and are often expected and accommodated in treatment plans. Interested readers should consult the work of Salekin and colleagues (2010).

While the above review was cursory, it illustrates the point that, at least for some, psychopathic states (or traits) are mutable or manageable. Whether this is owing to misdiagnosing psychopathy as a primary disorder and it is some underlying condition that is modifiable remains unclear. Further, it should be obvious at this point that the treatment should be multifaceted, addressing the home situation, pertinent relationships, as well as personal deficits and needs. At this time, no protocol is in place with respect to lines of treatment for psychopathy. However, several strategies are emerging, as briefly noted above, that offer direction and hope for the treatment of psychopathy. The following will briefly review emerging strategies and approaches under investigation that, while not differentiating by psychopathic variant (covered in Chapter 3), offer promise. These treatments can be thought of as part of a comprehensive treatment plan rather than as isolated strategies.

Recent Developments in Treatment for CU Traits

Since the publication of many of the early treatment studies, several new lines of work have focused more directly on callous–unemotional traits in youth and have yielded cautiously optimistic results. There is a growing literature aimed at identifying the active elements of interventions for adolescents with CU traits. Much of this work is targeted toward youth who have both, CU traits and conduct problems. For example, a recent narrative and systematic reviews of treatments for disruptive behavior and CU youth conclude that these traits are not uniformly treatment-refractory; Rather, findings indicate that outcomes are best when interventions start early, deliberately increase parental warmth and positive involvement, rely heavily on rewards and praise rather than punishment, and directly target emotion recognition and prosocial goal setting (e.g., Thomson, Kevorkian et al., 2025). This work also shifts the narrative away from therapeutic pessimism toward a more nuanced, risk- and needs-focused view of psychopathic-like features in youth.

A key development in this area has been the modification of existing parent training programs to better suit the specific social and emotional needs of children with callous-unemotional (CU) features. For example, Parent–Child Interaction Therapy has been modified to create PCIT-CU. This intervention keeps the core behavior management elements of PCIT, but adds a specific focus on increasing parental warmth, teaching emotional vocabulary, and using salient, reward-based approaches to encourage positive behavior. The approach seems promising. For example, a recent randomized controlled trial compared standard PCIT with the version adapted for CU traits in young children *with conduct problems* and found that both treatments reduced externalizing problems and CU traits. However, the CU-adapted version showed some advantages. Specifically, it was better at maintaining improvements in conduct problems at follow-up and at increasing positive parenting behaviors (Fleming et al., 2022). Related work, discussed further below, on PCIT protocols that target emotional development (e.g., PCIT-ED) likewise suggests that, when interventions explicitly address emotional competence and parent–child warmth, CU traits themselves can show meaningful decreases over time (Donohue et al., 2021).

Other novel formats also address the socioemotional deficits among youth with conduct disorder and CU traits. One such innovation is the use of immersive virtual reality (VR) to deliver brief socioemotional interventions. The Impact VR program, for example, exposes adolescents to emotionally charged interpersonal scenarios in a virtual environment and requires them to recognize emotional cues, consider others' perspectives, and choose prosocial responses. The early feasibility and acceptability studies and emerging randomized trials suggest that such VR-based interventions are acceptable to youth, can improve emotion recognition, and may reduce CU traits and conduct problems over short follow-up periods, although replication and longer-term data are still needed (Thomson, Kevorkian et al., 2025; Thomson, Perera et al., 2025; Schaarsberg et al., 2023).

In addition to the above, mentalization-based approaches originally developed for adolescents with emerging personality pathology have been adapted for youth with conduct disorder, and some have reported short-term reductions in aggression and antisocial behavior. Mentalization-Based Treatment for Conduct Disorder (MBT-CD), for instance, aims to improve the adolescent's capacity to understand behavior, both their own and that of others, in terms of underlying mental states. Early feasibility work indicates that MBT-CD is implementable and acceptable in youth with serious conduct problems, with preliminary evidence of reductions in aggression and externalizing symptoms (Taubner et al., 2021). This is relevant here owing to the overlap between CD or oppositional defiant disorder (ODD) can CU traits.

Although these interventions are not designed exclusively around psychopathy or CU traits, they reflect a broader movement toward mechanism-focused, developmentally informed treatment strategies that may be relevant for youth with psychopathic-like presentations.

The following sections review in more detail some of the foundational aspects of these approaches.

Comment Box: Variant-Specific Treatment Considerations

A particularly important development since the earlier work on psychotherapy for psychopathic traits concerns the role of variant differentiation in treatment response. As discussed in Chapter 3, youth with psychopathic-like features can present as primary (low anxiety, low emotional reactivity) or secondary (high anxiety, often trauma-linked), and these constellations may reflect different etiological pathways and therefore treatment needs. Historically, research has rarely examined whether treatments are equally effective across these variants, especially for younger children whose emotional capacities are still developing (Donohue et al., 2021). Recent work begins to address this gap.

A large randomized controlled trial evaluating Parent–Child Interaction Therapy–Emotion Development (PCIT-ED) in preschoolers (Donohue et al., 2021) incorporated this variant perspective directly into its rationale. Although the study did not formally subtype children, its sampling frame of clinically depressed preschoolers necessarily included youth who resemble the secondary, anxious variant, while prior research indicates that emotionally blunted, low-anxiety children approximating the primary variant may also be represented.

Importantly, CU traits did not interfere with treatment response for either depression or oppositionality, suggesting that anxious CU youth, contrary to longstanding assumptions, are not inherently treatment-resistant. Even more notable, PCIT-ED produced significant reductions in CU traits themselves, and these gains were maintained 18 weeks after treatment (Donohue et al., 2021).

Because emotional numbing and interpersonal disengagement appear to have different origins in primary versus secondary variants, this finding indicates that interventions targeting emotional development, parental warmth, affiliative bonding, and children's capacity to understand and respond to others' emotions may benefit both groups. For secondary-variant youth, these approaches may help recalibrate affective functioning shaped by trauma or chronic distress, while for primary-variant youth they may compensate for dispositional deficits in emotional responsivity and affiliative reward. *Though optimism must remain cautious here as traumatized or distressed youth may not have access to parents capable of engaging in an appropriate way.*

Taken together, these findings support the notion that treatment effectiveness should not be prematurely discounted for either variant. Rather, interventions that focus on early emotional competencies and parent–child connection appear promising across the psychopathy spectrum and represent an important direction for future treatment innovation.

Mental Models Approach

Mental models are in a very basic sense the parameters with which individuals guide their interpretations of the world. They represent the knowledge that people have about certain situations or things that individuals use to inform new ones. This all seems a bit abstract, but in the practical, the more ways you have to think about an issue, the more capable you are of broadening your interpretations of a situation or phenomenon and thus dealing with it. The more restricted an individual is in their mental models, the less apt they are to navigate new ways of interpreting things or solving problems leaving them more susceptible to inaccuracies and errors. In other words, the same solution does not fit every problem. If you only know one method to come to a solution, then you are very restricted in your approach to novel issues and with problem solving. Methods aimed at expanding your mental models (i.e., view of how the world works, assumptions, and expectations or tools for examining things) increase your ability to successfully navigate new situations and guide actions.

Attempts to modify beliefs and ideas among those youth with CU traits should focus specifically on transforming ideas that would otherwise lead to unhealthy withdrawal, aggressive or anti-social responses, and other complications. Evidence from recent research is instructive on this point. Though it was not presented as mental models research, it points to this approach's possible efficacy. Findings suggests that limiting exposure to witnessed violence may diminish violence among those with CU traits (Howard, Kimonis, Muñoz, & Frick, 2012). If a youth's mental model, for example, is saturated with ideas about using aggression to solve problems and that guides behavior, then exposure to violence may simply serve to reinforce those views. Hence, further direction for practitioners concerned with youth having risk factors for violence and delinquency, for example, may come from this mental models approach and limiting exposure to violence among those with CU traits specifically. While other paradigms may be used to inform the interpretation of these findings e.g., social learning, exposure to forms of symbolic reality, such as the media, can be a source of informing one's mental models. Arguably, the mental models approach shows promise (Salekin, Tippey, & Allen, 2012).

The efficacy of using mental models treatment with psychopathic youth has borne out in research. Specifically, Salekin and colleagues (2012) evaluated mental models intervention aimed at increasing motivation, raising positive emotion, and decreasing interpersonal callousness in youth having psychopathic CU traits. The program evinced promising results such that positive emotion increased through the treatment period, CU traits were reduced, and treatment amenability increased (Salekin, Tippey, & Allen, 2012).

While the above offered only a very cursory review at how the mental models approach may serve as a treatment protocol for youth with CU traits, initial results are promising. The basic idea is to transform the way that these youths perceive the world, the prescribed ways that they may respond to it, and the expectations that a youth may have about their reactions or responses to problems. This may look very different depending upon whether a youth is recognized to be a primary, not-anxious or secondary, anxious youth. A youth's background would also be telling as existing mental models would be, in part, shaped by prior experience, such as traumatic, negligent or even violent rearing and experiences. Mental models therapy would ideally assist youth, either primary or secondary, in transforming how they interpret the world, their expectations, and the ideas that predispose certain affect and behaviors. Certainly, proper training by clinicians before undertaking such therapy is warranted.

Since the initial Salekin et al. (2012) trial, there has been relatively little direct replication of mental models interventions with psychopathic-like youth, although the core idea of systematically reshaping expectations, beliefs, and response tendencies is increasingly reflected in newer socioemotional and cognitive-behavioral programs. Many of the more recent VR-based and emotion-recognition interventions, for example, can be viewed as updating youths' mental models about emotional cues, others' intentions, and the likely outcomes of aggressive versus prosocial actions, albeit under different labels (e.g., Thomson, Kevorkian et al., 2025; Thomson, Perera et al., 2025).

Cognitive Remediation

Cognitive remediation, simply stated, attempts to train individuals via targeted exercises in cognitive skills in the areas where deficiencies have been observed. There is a plethora of resources available on the topic more generally as the rehabilitation method has been used in the service of multiple disorders, e.g., memory, attention, language and or executive function disorders. The treatment is meant as an adjunct to other medical and or psychotherapeutic treatments.

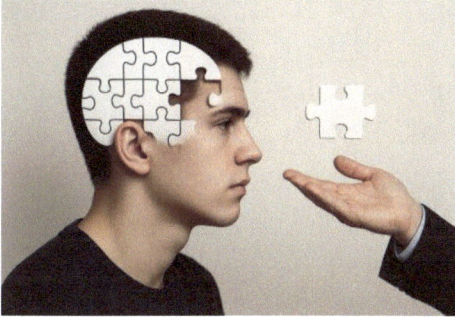

Cognitive remediation recently has been offered in attempts to target deficits seen with psychopathy (Baskin-Sommers, Curtin, & Newman, 2015). Specifically, researchers sought to examine the efficacy of this treatment for two anti-social subtypes, those individuals with psychopathy that fail to consider contextual information and those exhibiting externalizing traits featuring cognitive-affective problems thought to lead to significant substance abuse and criminal behavior. With emphasis on those identified as being psychopathic, the researchers relied on previous research that suggested that the psychopath's impairment rests with their reduced ability to consider multiple streams of information simultaneously (i.e., early attention bottleneck), but instead, relevant information is processed serially. In circumstances with many distractions, this ability to serially filter can be viewed as an advantage. However, this tendency is problematic when it results in a failure to simultaneously process important information conflicting with goal-oriented behavior.

The psychopath's affective and inhibitory deficits are contingent on whether the information to be processed is consistent with their goal (i.e., cognitive-affective deficit in *attention to context,* ATC). The researchers note that this, "..results in a myopic perspective on decision making and goal-directed behavior, such that individuals with psychopathy are adept at using information that is directly relevant to their goal to effectively regulate behavior (e.g., modulate behavior and ignore emotions to con someone), but display impulsive behavior (e.g., quitting one's job in the absence of an alternative one) and egregious

decision making (e.g., seeking publicity for a con while wanted by po-
lice) when information is beyond their immediate focus of attention"
(Baskin-Sommers et al., 2015, p. 46).

Improvement in these deficits was realized from the offered 1
hour per week, 6-week training in ATC, which focused on learning to
attend to and integrate environmental context cues (p. 49). The authors
believe that such findings point to potential for new types of deficit-
matched interventions. While this treatment modality is still novel in
the present context (but has gained *some* traction), these results are
certainly promising and may present as an important adjunct to other
treatments.

Since the original ATC training work, there are some researchers
who have continued to explore how CU traits relate to cognitive control and reward sensitivity, with several reviews suggesting that CU
traits are associated with distinctive patterns of executive functioning
and responsivity to reward and punishment (Pauli-Pott, Sens, & Pott,
2025). However, to date there have been few large-scale efforts to directly extend ATC-style cognitive remediation to adolescents with
pronounced CU traits. At present, cognitive remediation for psychopathic-like features remains a promising but still emerging adjunct,
with the strongest empirical foundation currently in adult samples and
in broader disruptive behavior disorders rather than in CU-focused
youth trials. Interested readers are urged to consult the work of Baskin-
Sommers and colleagues (2015) and Pauli-Pott, Sens, and Pott (2025).

Pharmaceutical Therapy

There has been recent movement in formally testing the use of
Clozapine in the treatment of ASPD in adults and conduct disorder in

youth. Clozapine is an anti-psychotic drug that has proven to be useful owning to its anti-aggressive properties in the treatment of schizophrenia and in other personality disorders, i.e., borderline personality disorder (Brown et al., 2014). Currently, this is a novel approach for psychopathy, but one that shows some promise. However, studies at this point are too limited to draw definitive conclusions.

For one study, investigators looked at the efficacy of using Clozapine in 7 patients with primary ASPD and high psychopathic traits (Brown et al., 2014). These patients were housed at a UK based high-security hospital and demonstrated a significant history of serious vio-

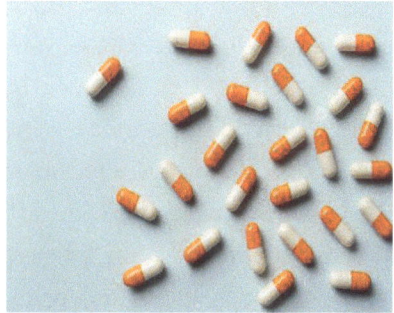

lence. After administration of the drug, patients showed meaningful improvement in all domains of the disorder, with the most significant gains in the area of impulse-behavioral control and anger. The drug also acted to reduce the number of violent acts committed by these patients. These gains were realized using lower doses of the drug (serum levels < 350 ng/m). Interested readers are encouraged to review Brown et al., (2014).

In another study, Clozapine was used in adolescents exhibiting severe conduct disorder (Teixeira et al., 2013). Here, seven boys between the ages of 10 to 14 who had failed other types of interventions and treatments were administered Clozapine and evaluated over 26 weeks. Marked control of symptoms were noted, and the researchers found good tolerance of the drug in doses between 100-600 mg/day.

Even with these findings, certainly study is limited. There is also a real unease about extending this type of therapy to youth, and anti-psychotic drugs are attached to significant side effects. With these concerns in mind, there likely will be continued interest in using pharmaceutical therapy as a line of treatment. It is also likely that these and similar drugs are already used in practice.

Subsequent work has largely reinforced the view that pharmacological strategies should be framed as targeting aggression and comorbid conditions (e.g., ADHD, mood disorders) rather than psychopathy itself. Systematic reviews of medication for aggression in conduct disorder indicate that stimulants, certain atypical antipsychotics, and mood stabilizers can reduce aggressive behavior in youth, including some with CU traits, but CU traits do not consistently predict stronger or weaker response to medication (Balia et al., 2018; see also Pisano & Masi, 2020; Zagórski et al., 2025). At the same time, there have been no large, controlled trials of clozapine or other antipsychotics specifically for youth identified primarily on the basis of CU traits or psychopathic features. As a result, despite suggestive case series in highly aggressive adolescents, pharmacological approaches remain adjunctive and symptom-focused, and must be weighed carefully against their considerable side-effect profiles as noted, especially when contemplated for younger populations.

In sum, given the above reviewed approaches and therapies, however limited, it appears that the movement in this area is promising and counters the idea that effective treatments cannot be or should not be devised for psychopathy. It is also worth emphasizing that if a youth's psychopathic *state* is the result of some other condition, such as emotional numbing or disassociation, as reviewed in Chapter 3, then treatment of the primary condition should be quite helpful overall. Therapy would then need to be tailored to the originating problems as identified though some assessment strategy, such as RNR. Finally, other strategies show promise for future development that were not discussed here and are touched upon in Chapter 6, e.g., epigenetics.

CHAPTER 4 MAIN POINTS

❖ There is reason to instigate treatment of those deemed psychopathic irrespective of sentiment that there is no treatment.

❖ Treatment of juvenile psychopathy appears possible, while attempts at differential diagnosis are quite reasonable in this context.

❖ Determining whether a youth has a psychopathic *trait* or *state* is important in discerning treatment needs, and using the framework of primary vs. secondary may be helpful toward that end.

❖ Intervention should begin early, focus on the area of greatest need, which is typically the parent or caregiver-youth relationship.

❖ Treatment strategies common to other settings and disorders are being tried with psychopathic or psychopathic-like youth with some success.

❖ Treatment strategies such as the mental models approach and cognitive remediation may prove to be important therapeutic adjuncts.

CHAPTER 5

LEGAL ISSUES RELATED TO DIAGNOSING YOUTH WITH PSYCHOPATHY

As noted in previous chapters, psychopaths are over-represented in the criminal justice system, whether they are primary or secondary, youth or adult. Some estimates, for example, place them as accounting for up to 25% of incarcerated adult and youthful offenders. Given such representation, research examining the consequences of a psychopathy diagnosis from criminal justice and civil court decision makers deserves discussion (see e.g., Morse, 2008). While much research into this area deals specifically with adult offenders, the fact that youth can be direct filed or waived into the adult courts makes such findings quite relevant.

It appears that a reasonable amount of confusion concerning juvenile psychopathy is an artifact of some of the measurement concerns previously discussed. Other problems result from some preconceived ideas shared by decision makers (e.g., Smith et al., 2014), as well as the accuracy of assessment devices used to guide criminal and civil decisions. While researchers and clinicians will employ various tactics and measures to conduct studies and provide treatment, the use of these devices by court actors is another matter altogether. For youth, even more hesitancy surrounds the use of these tools because the consequences can be so grave. One concern surrounds the potential for false-positives. That is applying a label of psychopath (or APSD -some use these terms interchangeably) to a youth that is not one. This becomes important to the legal context as being identified as psychopathic, whether they are or not, is associated with increased criminality and future predicted risk. Potentially elevated consequences may therefore be attached to these individuals as the courts misuse information meant for the clinical context. These concerns are shared among many. In fact, in a 2025 note in the Harvard Law Review, the level of alarm is palpable concerning using the ASPD label, "..the modern incarnation of the "psychopathic personality" in the courts (Harvard Law Review, 2025, p. 1101).

As remarked concerning the APSD/psychopathy construct:

> *Mental health professionals must also realize that a disclaimer in the DSM does not go far enough to protect against the way the legal system interprets and applies clinical knowledge. Clinical and legal professionals must learn from the past and work against perpetuating biases and harmful self-fulfilling prophecies.*

Harvard Law Review, 2025, p. 1122

The Courts and Psychopathy in U.S. Legal Context: A Brief History

To better understand the current use of psychopathy by the courts (and how it can be applied to juveniles), it is important to briefly review the legal history. For essentially a century in the US, the use of psychopathy has been legally relevant, with one of the earliest examples seen with the case *Carter v. State* (1927). In that case, which was a death penalty case involving an alleged serial killer, the examining physician described defendant Frank Carter (an adult) as a psychopathic personality. The Nebraska Supreme Court affirmed his death sentence as the label was used as evidence of a *morally disordered* and *dangerous character*. Thus, even prior to all contemporary studies on the issue and apart from modern risk assessment instruments, the courts have accepted psychopathy as a meaningful indicator of future violence and impaired moral sensibility.

Similar reasoning appeared in state cases involving *psychopathic personalities* and *sex psychopath* statutes throughout the middle of the last century. Although the terminology predated DSM classifications, judges routinely viewed psychopathic traits as indicators of persistent dangerousness that justified indeterminate commitments or enhanced sentencing. These early cases served to lay the groundwork for today's legal reliance on psychopathy.

It is in the modern era that the construct became more formalized with the development of psychopathy quantifiers, particularly the Hare Psychopathy Checklist–Revised (PCL-R), allowing psychopathy to enter the courtroom as a measurable risk factor. Courts now increasingly use PCL-R scores to support arguments about recidivism, volitional impairment, and the need for incapacitation. This extends to statutes such as New York's Article 10 civil-management scheme (i.e., Article 10 of the New York Mental Hygiene Law (MHL), 2007), which is one of the clearest contemporary examples of psychopathy influencing legal outcomes. This civil commitment statute (and others like it) requires proof of a mental abnormality that predisposes an individual to sexual offending and creates serious difficulty controlling behavior (https://www.nysenate.gov/legislation/laws/MHY/TBA10). Without getting too far into the litigation and discussion surrounding such statutes, and this one specifically, NY courts have consistently held that solely relying on antisocial personality disorder (ASPD), for instance, is insufficient to meet the standard. When it is combined with psychopathic traits or elevated PCL-R scores, however, the statutory standard is frequently met (e.g., *Matter of State of New York v. Anthony L.*, 2017). As seen in cases such as *Matter of State of New York v. Kareem M.* (2018) and *Matter of Dennis K.* (2010/2011), psychopathy often functions as the decisive factor distinguishing routine criminality from a legally cognizable mental abnormality warranting civil confinement. This is the orientation in many similar types of statutes and cases. For those interested, the Supreme Court addressed such statutes in *Kansas v. Hendericks* (1997).

These examples from history demonstrate that psychopathy has served as a powerful legal proxy for indicating dangerousness and further highlights its continuing role as a risk-amplifying construct in American law. Juveniles become subject in like way as the courts have signaled their acceptance of using psychopathy in the legal context. At the same time, current clinical and empirical findings challenge the reliability, validity and fairness of psychopathy-linked risk assessments (and other evaluation instruments) to the point that the ethics of their use by the courts are in real question. Problematically, the influence of such evaluation tools persists despite ongoing debates about scientific validity.

Risk Assessment in General

As briefly touched upon in the chapter on treatment, assessment tools have become commonplace for use by the courts. Problematically, there are issues with accurate prediction, as noted, despite the commendable goal of public safety. In fact, while there are many comparative reviews of screening tools available, tools which are notorious for producing false-positives, it appears that these devices do much better at predicting low risk than anything else. For example, in research evaluating the efficacy of 9 of the most common screening tools to predict violence, sexual violence and criminal behavior, scholars looked at 73 samples involving 24,827 people from 13 countries (Fazel, Singh, Doll, & Grann, 2012). The screening tools analyzed in this representative study are listed in Table 5.1. Included are the PCL-R and the Structured Assessment of Violence Risk in Youth (SAVRY), which is aimed at adolescent offenders.

While the screening tools did well at predicting low risk with high accuracy, there were problems when it came to identifying risk particular to context. Specifically, there was performance heterogeneity of the tools tied to the intent of the assessment; if the tools were used to inform treatment and management, then these performed moderately well when predicting violence and general offending (p. 4). However, when a tool was used exclusively for sentencing and related decisions (probation, parole and release), then their worth was limited (p. 4). The authors caution that, based on their findings, these tools cannot be used to prognosticate about individual level of risk for repeat offending, particularly when used alone. Such findings provide an example of recurrent sentiments in the literature despite the certain desirability to predict risk (see also Argueta-Cevallos, 2021; DeMatteo & Olver, 2022; Fazel et al., 2022 for further discussion), and the concern is not going away.

Table 5.1 Risk assessment tools evaluated by Fazel et al., 2012	
Actuarial	
Level of Service Inventory-Revised (LSI-R)	Andrews & Bonita, 1995
Psychopathy Checklist-Revised (PCL-R)	Hare, 1991, 2003
Sex Offender Risk Appraisal Guide (SORAG)	Quinsey et al., 1998, 2006
Static-99	Harris et al., 2003
Violence Risk Appraisal Guide (VRAG)	Quinsey et al., 1998, 2006
Structured Clinical Judgment	
Historical, Clinical, Risk Management-20 (HCR-20)	Webster et al., 1995, 1997
Sexual Violence Risk-20 (SVR-20)	Boer et al., 1997
Spousal Assault Risk Assessment (SARA)	Kropp et al., 1994, 1995, 1999
Structured Assessment of Violence Risk in Youth (SAVRY)	Borum, Bartel, & Forth, 2002, 2003
Note: Modified from Table 1, Fazel et al., 2012, p. 8. For interested readers, the paper is available at: https://www.bmj.com/content/345/bmj.e4692	

Without presenting a comprehensive review of the assessment tools noted here and the over 100 others with their respective evaluations (e.g., DeMatteo & Olver, 2022; Fazel et al., 2022; Viljoen, Cochrane, & Jonnson, 2018), it can be said with reasonable confidence that we simply are not there yet as many studies continue to produce similar findings. It is equally important to note that reliability and accuracy in research does not mean it is accurate and reliable enough to be applied in legal settings. This remains a common and costly misconception and reflects a broader tension between scientific standards and the heightened precision demanded in legal contexts. The authors of the example study reviewed above said it nicely when stating that, "even after 30 years of development, the view that violence, sexual, or criminal risk can be predicted in most cases is not evidence based. This message is important to the public, media, and some administrations who may have unrealistic expectations of risk prediction for clinicians" (Fazel et al., 2012, p. 5). More recent studies echo this sentiment, e.g., Fazel et al., 2022. Obviously, nothing is certain. This is readily apparent for youth, many of whom tend to desist as they age (e.g., age-crime curve). Along with the intent to limit risk to others, there is also a cost joined to those predicted to be violent or criminal who ultimately fall into the false-positive group. These costs are also borne by the tax-payers who pay for their potentially enhanced confinement and management.

Of note, the PCL-R is regularly used in criminal justice settings, and its use is only growing (see DeMatteo & Olver, 2022). Problematically and realistically, the training often falls short of that needed for proper application of the instrument. On this point, Hare (2016) offers that one of the problems of its use is related to the adversarial nature of the proceedings such that defense and prosecutor witnesses will present very different PCL-R scores. He instructs that one way to circumvent this is to require extensive training of such witnesses. Since the juvenile courts in the U.S. are not adversarial, but a number of youth are waived to adult courts, recognition of this tendency contributes to this discussion and adds to the above concerns to the extent that they are applicable.

Risk Assessment for Youth and Psychopathy

Although issues of reliability and accuracy remain, contemporary juvenile justice risk instruments intentionally exclude psychopathy measures, or try to, for many reasons already discussed or will be addressed in the following sections. Among them, developmental science strongly cautions against labelling adolescents with psychopathic traits due to high instability of personality features during adolescence and the potential for iatrogenic harm (recall the age limit on diagnosing a youth). Additionally, tools like the Youth Assessment and Screening Instrument (YASI) are founded on the RNR model (discussed in the previous chapter), which prioritizes dynamic risk factors amenable to intervention (Orbis Partners, Inc, 2007), whereas psychopathy arguably reflects a relatively stable personality construct. Including psychopathy indicators would therefore conflict with the rehabilitative focus of juvenile systems. Youth psychopathy assessments, too, such as the Psychopathy Check List -Youth Version (PCL-YV; Forth, Kosson, & Hare, 2003) scoring, introduce substantial ethical concerns, including stigma, poor inter-rater reliability in non-research settings, and disproportionate impacts on minority youth. Finally, agencies often avoid psychopathy measures to reduce litigation risks, since some courts have been highly critical of using such labels to justify punitive outcomes for minors.

Unlike the YASI, the PCL-YV is a *clinically oriented* measure designed to assess a specific constellation of affective, interpersonal, and lifestyle traits associated with psychopathy (e.g., shallow affect, callousness, deceitfulness, manipulativeness). The PCL-YV relies on file review and semi-structured interview data to evaluate theoretically grounded facets of psychopathy, many of which are developmentally sensitive and can be considered controversial when applied to adolescents. In contrast, the YASI is an actuarial risk/needs tool intended for case planning, not personality assessment. It measures dynamic factors that can change with intervention and does not evaluate the affective or interpersonal dimensions central to psychopathy. Thus, while both instruments may touch on antisocial behavior, they represent fundamentally different frameworks, one diagnostic and trait-oriented (PCL-YV) and the other managerial and risk-oriented (YASI).

The YASI does not escape scrutiny concerning its reliability and generalizability, however, and particularly when it comes to representing all demographic groups (e.g., Matz, Martinez, & Kujava, 2021). For example, Matz, Martinez, and Kujava's (2021) examination of North Dakota juvenile probationers found only moderate predictive accuracy for general reoffending (AUC = .66), with notably weaker performance among girls and unclear validity for African American and Native American youth. The point on reliability made earlier also resonates here; that is, reliability in research and clinical settings does not translate to legal contexts. The standards and consequences are very different.

There is also concern over the YASI's conceptual overlap with the psychopathy construct (see Comment Box: Overlap Between YASI Domains and Psychopathy). Although the YASI does not contain psychopathy scales or callous–unemotional items, it includes constructs such as empathy, impulse control, aggression, compliance, and antisocial attitudes, and this is where the problems in this context rest. These domains, while framed as criminogenic needs within the RNR model, mirror several behavioral components used historically to index psychopathy in youth (e.g., impulsivity, irresponsibility, rule-breaking). Consequently, the YASI may inadvertently capture *behavioral correlates* of psychopathy without measuring the affective–interpersonal features that define the construct. Such observations raise additional ethical concerns about attributing risk to traits that resemble psychopathic characteristics when the YASI was never designed to, nor validated for, assessing psychopathy.

Comment Box:
Overlap Between YASI Domains and Psychopathy

Although the YASI does not include psychopathy scales or items assessing callous–unemotional traits, several of its domain (e.g., impulsivity, empathy problems, attitudes toward delinquency, aggression, and behavioral noncompliance) overlap conceptually with behavioral components that appear in some youth psychopathy research. These similarities reflect broad criminogenic needs rather than the affective–interpersonal features that define psychopathy. Nevertheless, the overlap can complicate interpretation when YASI scores are used to guide supervision, placement, or intervention decisions, because elevated scores may be mistakenly treated as indicators of deeper personality disturbance when the instrument was not designed for that purpose.

Concerns about interpretive accuracy are further heightened by research indicating inconsistencies in the YASI's predictive performance across demographic groups and jurisdictions. For example, Matz and colleagues (2021) found that in North Dakota the YASI demonstrated only moderate predictive accuracy for general reoffending and performed notably weaker for females than males. The authors also emphasized the need for further evaluation among African American and Native American youth, for whom predictive validity could not be firmly established. Together, these findings underscore that, despite its broad adoption, the YASI's accuracy varies, and any conceptual overlap with psychopathy-adjacent behavioral traits warrants cautious interpretation. The YASI was not created to measure psychopathy, has never been validated as such, and cannot substitute tools specifically designed to assess psychopathic traits.

Risk, Criminal Institutionalization, and Differential Criminality

In an earlier chapter, variants of psychopathy were discussed that have a bearing on the present context. There are some differences observed between the variants that make it to formal intervention in the criminal justice system compared to the non-confined or non-adjudicated. Primary youth under confinement are likely scoring much higher in CU traits than those in the community. Another fundamental difference between the confined offender samples used in research and the noninstitutionalized is the co-occurring volatile behavior that was troublesome enough to bring these youth to the attention of the authorities. With this in mind, research alerts to the idea that the secondary variant is more likely to harbor a number of features (e.g., impulsivity, vulnerability to peers, aggression, etcetera) that place them *at risk* for volatility and subsequent incarceration (Camp et al., 2013; Flexon, 2015; Skeem et al., 2003). Such risk factors have long been recognized in the criminology literature, and are commonly organized by domains, including individual (e.g., biological and psychological dispositions, attitudes, values, knowledge, skills, problem behaviors); peer (e.g., norms, activities, attachment); family (e.g., function, management, bonding, abuse/violence); school (e.g., bonding, climate, policy, performance); and community (e.g., bonding, norms, resources, poverty level, crime) (Development Services Group, Inc., 2015, p. 2). These risk factors vary in significance depending upon developmental age. Interested readers on this point and for more detailed information concerning the breakdown of risk (and protective) factors are encouraged to visit the OJJDP publication on risk factors available at https://ojjdp.ojp.gov/library/publications/risk-and-protective-factors-child-delinquency.

It is interesting that many of these risk factors, which are often used by the courts, are argued to be developmentally important to secondary psychopathy. Some of these are interchangeable in terms of risk and are not additive in effect (Flexon & Meldrum, 2013). While the primary variant may have some of these risk factors, theory and research indicates a more idiopathic course than argued for the secondary variant. Including all of those scoring high on psychopathy in research to delineate risks may then confound attempts to understand how these associated vulnerabilities attach to psychopathy and externalizing behaviors. Such aggregation also confounds the courts' attempts to secure clarity in decisions.

The above idea comports with research showing a lack of association for youth resembling the primary variant (solely having CU traits) and instrumental aggression, which may reflect a deficit rather than a surplus of motivation (Camp et al., 2013, p. 11). Such findings may point to the idea that absent other drivers (covariates of aggression and or anti-sociality) or co-morbid conditions, youth who are solely callous and unemotional are not particularly aggressive or violent. For example, some incarcerated primary youth in one study were found to have a history of maternal neglect, an extra element to CU traits (Kimonis et al., 2013). Nested in findings from the above and other research examining noninstitutionalized primary youth, it appears some-

thing in addition to CU traits may be promoting criminally linked behavior. This point does not refute an association between CU traits and
a variety of other actions including anti-social behaviors that are not
criminal.

In like way, findings suggest that the secondary variant, known to
have scores that are slightly lower on CU traits than primary youth,
exhibit trait anxiety and are vulnerable to characteristics (i.e., impulsivity; dis-inhibitory traits) that promote criminal behavior (Camp et
al., 2013). It is important to note again that some have connected the
primary variant specifically with the affective deficits (Factor 1, affective facet) of psychopathy and less impulsivity (Factor 2, lifestyle facet) than secondary psychopaths (Skeem et al., 2003, p. 529). Thus, co-
morbid conditions, risks and vulnerabilities may underlie the secondary psychopathic-like youth's association with anti-sociality (Seagrave
& Grisso, 2002) but is not absolute. For example, in statistical models
examining CU traits and anxiety, once other covariates are added, an
association with aggressive behavior is diminished. This indicates that
other conditions that are associated with the secondary variant may
partially drive the association with anti-social behavior (Flexon, 2015,
2016), and it may be that this suggested differential risk for criminal
behavior is obscured by research that treats psychopathy in a homogeneous way.

Unfortunately, research further elucidating the above points concerning specifically psychopathy is lacking. The situation also is quite
messy and circular. Research from many forensic samples inform what
is known about psychopathy, which is then used to identify youth who
may be psychopathic. However, many identified as psychopathic may
have co-morbid conditions that can lend to scoring high on CU traits.
Manifestations from the co-morbid conditions may result in youth being brought to the attention of authorities, which draws them into the

criminal justice system, which is diagnostic of psychopathy using some instruments. However, these youths may present as false-positives of psychopathy, while at the same time informing further research used by clinicians and the courts because criminal behavior is being used as an indicator for psychopathy.

Legal Consequences: Psychopathy, the Courts, and Culpability

For the concerns here, it matters less that the psychopathy diagnosis is necessarily accurate, but more so that it was made in the first place and whether any additional legal consequences attach to the label. Once the label is applied in an official setting and it is tied to criminal anti-sociality, ramifications to the *psychopathic* individual have the potential to be quite costly. Some may view disparate treatment of those deemed psychopathic as a positive thing; The system manages such offenders who arguably have no known treatment and may be a continuing societal threat. The individual is taken off the street so to speak. Yet, if the label is misapplied, then some individuals are paying a price for being tied to a condition that they may or may not have. For these individuals, inaccurately labeled and otherwise, the question also arises whether and how they should be held culpable for a condition beyond their control (Morse, 2008) or whether and what kinds of treatment will be offered.

This is not to say that people do not deserve punishment for their behaviors. Nonetheless, caution is reasonable because individuals may be receiving more (or less) punishment than they deserve owning to a diagnosis of psychopathy and or may not be receiving a warranted treatment. Since justice is defined as equity, fairness, impartiality, and neutrality, and punishment is discerned principally on culpability, the impact of psychopathy on criminal justice decision makers rests in how psychopathy is conceived. Does it make them more, less or equally culpable? The following examines how criminal justice decision makers may treat such evidence in the courts and if preexisting beliefs and attitudes related to psychopathy may inform decisions in a way that can impact juveniles.

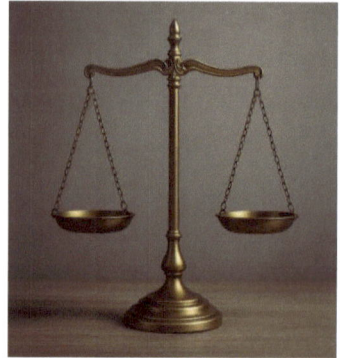

The Brian Dugan case presents an interesting illustration in this context. Although Dugan is an adult and his case was a death penalty case, lessons can be gleaned concerning how offering evidence of mental defect via a psychopathy diagnosis can play out. It is important to note upfront that juveniles cannot be formally diagnosed with a personality disorder until they reach age 18 and cannot be given a death sentence for crimes committed under that same age, but the case is instructive as it gives some insight about how evidence of psychopathic tendencies might play out.

Dugan was found guilty of raping and murdering little girls and was already serving life sentences. Sparing the details of his crimes and victims, Dugan confessed to another rape and murder in which the prosecution sought the death penalty. The defense offered brain scan (fMRI) evidence in addition to expert testimony at sentencing to support the idea that Dugan's brain was consistent with a finding of psychopathy and this diminished his culpability. In essence, the argument was that psychopaths have different brains that fail to inhibit them from acting in anti-social ways, much like that seen with other mental defects. Though the effort was intended to mitigate a capital sentence and outweigh the aggravators, the jury came back with a death penalty decision. Some observers have suggested that the jury deliberated much longer than they would have had such evidence not been offered, since they asked to re-read the testimony on the neuroscience. The testimony also included those experts that disagreed with the conclusions of the fMRI evidence. In the end, it appears that the jury granted less weight to the evidence for mitigation purposes.

It is important emphasize again that the Dugan case was a death penalty case, which is most often bifurcated into two stages, a guilt phase and a sentencing phase (some are trifurcated). In the sentencing phase, there is a tendency to offer more latitude with respect to the types of evidence that are allowed, and in many jurisdictions jurors must weigh and sort through (at times tenuous) aggravating against mitigating evidence. So, with this in mind, fMRI scans for psychopathy may not be up to the evidentiary standards used in the guilt phase or non-capital trials. However, expert testimony with respect to psychiatric conditions is generally allowed at trial and is common in pre-sentence investigation (PSI) reports, which are given to judges to make sentencing decisions, and used at other stages of the criminal justice system.

While it is not known whether and how the evidence presented in the Dugan case was instrumental in the jurors' decision to vote for death, some research suggests that evidence supporting a diagnosis of psychopathy in death cases serves as an aggravating circumstance. Just as seen in the Dugan case, findings support the notion that evidence of psychopathy in a capital case may lend to decisions for death. This may indicate that jurors or other criminal justice decision makers will render severe punishments when indications of psychopathy or emerging psychopathy is evoked irrespective of the defense's intent for mitigation.

Pertinent to this discussion is that some jurisdictions require a finding from the jury of future dangerousness (e.g., Texas). That is, the jury must make a finding that the convicted defendant will likely pose a continuing threat to society before they can render a death decision in a capital case. Introducing such evidence from the perspective of the defense should be made very thoughtfully. It is one thing to introduce evidence with the argument that a defendant is less responsible because of mental defect. The intent here is obviously mitigation. Problematically, the mental defect argument is tied to a diagnosis that most often carries with it a belief that it is immutable and tied to persistent criminality and anti-sociality. This opens the door to the ultimate penal sanction via statute alone, not simply through pre-existing prejudices. The most often relied upon measurement tool for psychopathy ties behavior to the diagnosis. If the evidence of psychopathy is introduced by the prosecution, such evidence is likely beneficial to the state's cause. Moreover, such arguments that have insinuations of future dangerousness extend to non-death penalty cases. These innuendo by prosecutors of future dangerousness (e.g., cold-blooded, evil) are intended to remind jurors of a continuing threat to society that they can thwart through conviction decisions.

While the juvenile death penalty was struck as unconstitutional in 2005 (*Roper v. Simmons*, 2005), this reality obviously does not mean that youth diagnosed with psychopathy or suggested to have psychopathy via surrogate terminology escape severe punishment. There also is a concern that indicators of juvenile psychopathy will be used later on in adult life to inform criminal proceedings. Given that the introduction of evidence is nested in its probative value and potential to be prejudicial, issues related to the validity of the diagnostic tools used by professionals also come into play. A significant amount of discussion has already been made on this point in the previous chapters.

Adding to the complexity of the above, some research suggests that the impact of a psychopathy diagnosis on sentencing is nested in what type of evidence is presented to the court. One study found, for instance, that if a judge accepted that biomechanical processes caused the psychopathy, it would serve to mitigate their sentence (Aspinwall et al., 2012). Here, the biomechanical evidence, which appeared to increase the proportion of judges listing mitigating factors in their decisions, lessoned the perceived culpability of the offender. Granted, the study used a hypothetical case with expert testimony concerning a fake convict's psychopathy. Also, the real judges used in the study are trained professionals, but many decision makers that discern the fate of offenders are not. Rather, juries and other actors often make important decisions with respect to an offender's fate. Such deference to neurobiological or biomechanical evidence therefore may not extend beyond judges. Further, it is unknown whether and to what extent being a juvenile impacts decisions. Does being younger actually work against the youth because of the notion that psychopathic-like youth present a continuing threat with poor prognosis?

Human decision makers often rely on schemas to inform decisions, which begs the question, is there a *symbolic psychopathic assailant*? That is, a preconceived image of the evil psychopathic offender who seeks to prey upon others without remorse. It is possible, and it may influence certain actor's decisions regarding youth deemed psychopathic. Potential jurors very often identify psychopaths with infamous serial killers, mass murderers, and fictionalized killers, and they tend to get most of their information about psychopathy from movies and television (Smith et al., 2014). Such information has the potential to bias jurors and other decision makers as soon as the word *psychopathy* comes into play.

It is widely known that prosecutors use terms to describe offenders in order to create a picture in the minds of jurors, such as cold-blooded, heartless, and ruthless, as mentioned above. Such descriptions may be taken as synonymous with psychopathy by some jurors and result in augmented sentencing in the same way that being labelled a psychopath is associated with death sentencing. In a similar manner, non-capital jurors often are primed to think of issues related to future dangerousness, whether expected to do so by statute or not. If a juror or other decision maker believes that someone is by virtue of psychopathy a continuing threat, then their decisions will likely serve that belief. Since youth are the concern here, the impact of juror bias would only apply to youth who were direct filed or waived to adult courts. However, it is reasonable to assume that some juvenile justice personnel would be subject to similar biases as noted above. This is particularly true since youth services actors think of risk in terms of searching for treatment and meeting needs, whereas legal actors' focus shifts to their duty to protect the public. Hence, risk is thought of in very different ways depending upon the roles filled in this context that determine who is responsible to whom. [As an aside, this tension was readily apparent during a juvenile justice seminar recently attended by the author. Yet, neither side, youth services staff or the prosecutor in this setting, could truly appreciate the disconnect over how they viewed risk].

Juvenile courts are backlogged and stressed for resources. The introduction of screening devices that claim to afford the ability to predict future dangerousness and determine the efficacy of rehabilitation efforts for particular offenders are therefore desirable, but the combination of factors noted above presents a serious, potential threat. Psychopathy screening tools have the aura of being scientific and reliable in youth because they are trusted for research with much attention being paid to determining their validity and accuracy. However, identifying tendencies and statistical associations in research is different than predicting an individual's present needs and future tendencies. Additionally, the accuracy in practical applications is nonetheless in question precisely because these screening tools are being applied to youth who demonstrate transient features and states. This concern has been echoed as far back as Cleckley (1976, p. 270) and persists to present day.

To illustrate:

> ... were one to identify behaviors and attitudes consistent with psychopathy at a given point in time for a given youth, one may be observing characteristics of a future psychopathic adult. But there is a risk that one may be observing instead a transient feature of a developmental process characteristic of the youth as he or she reaches adult maturity... Clinicians ultimately will be responsible for knowing the likelihood that their observations of a youth's psychopathic-behaviors and attitudes are indicative of psychopathy (a true positive) or a transient product of a developmental process (a false positive).

Seagrave & Grisso, 2002, p. 224

Irrespective of strides in research, problems persist and the sentiment towards caution is echoed in more contemporary scholarship. Much of this research deals with examining stability of psychopathy over time. To some extent, this is done to determine if future behavior can be reliably predicted, which is a concern of the courts and for determining needs related to rehabilitative effort. Unfortunately, we are not at a place where confidence should be given to the ability to predict outcomes. As scholars have noted, "Given the importance placed on the construct of psychopathy across a number of contexts, such as legal decision making and treatment planning, it is important to emphasize that we still know relatively little about what factors predict persistence in these features over time" (Hawes et al., 2014, p. 632). To date, these observations hold. Issues of stability have already been discussed, but it is worth emphasizing here that some youth who score as psychopathic do not score as psychopathic as an adult. In like way, it is a typical pattern for youth to desist or age-out of their problematic behaviors, which appears to work in tandem with their aging out of psychopathy. Such findings point to problems with the assessment of psychopathy in youth, such as determining whether we are tapping into co-morbid conditions or behaviors that lend to a psychopathy diagnosis that is ultimately in error and discerning which features are states or traits.

A number of reasons can confound attempts to accurately identify and predict future behaviors. Some of these have been addressed in the research on desistance from crime, e.g., psychosocial maturation, bonding and commitment costs, assortative mating, etcetera. Strategies aimed at impression management in adolescence are also important here as youth embroiled in the juvenile or criminal justice systems likely present various façades to deal with the stresses of being chronically evaluated. How they present themselves may directly interfere with attempts at evaluation and risk assessment.

Ultimately, there are real problems when attempting to assess youth for psychopathy or psychopathic-like tendencies and for using this information for legal decision making. Owning to the belief that psychopathy is largely untreatable and presents as a risk for serious, chronic and violent offending, legal decision makers may react more punitively in the presence of such evidence depending upon how it is presented and whether it is used for treatment or other criminal justice decisions. Against a backdrop of imprecise risk assessment and a threat of false-positives, it would be prudent to take pause.

CHAPTER 5 MAIN POINTS

❖ Those deemed psychopathic are overrepresented in the criminal justice system, whether youth or adult, and this can be tied to a number of problematic reasons.

❖ Use of assessment tools as the sole determinant of risk for informing the courts should be avoided.

❖ False-positives for youth owning to risk assessment is especially problematic as the consequences can be initially serious and have the potential to be used against them as they age.

❖ Irrespective of predicted risk, youth are known to desist or age-out of troublesome behavior.

❖ Evidence of psychopathy or psychopathic-like tendencies can be used against youth rather than mitigate or lesson perceived culpability because it is often tied to fears of future dangerousness.

❖ Measurement issues are tied to legal issues in a circular fashion.

CHAPTER 6

DIRECTIONS FOR INFORMING CRIMINOLOGICAL THOUGHT AND FUTURE RESEARCH

Placing Psychopathy among Other Known Criminological

Correlates

First off, it seems appropriate to discuss what is meant by criminology. Criminology is a discipline involved with the study of crime and criminal behavior. People hold doctorates in criminology and criminal justice and study, among other things, the nature of crime and criminality using various levels of analysis and interdisciplinary understandings. For the sake of clarity here, a criminologist is someone with a terminal degree (Ph.D.) in criminology and or criminal justice. The field is interdisciplinary and requires extensive study just as any other. At the same time, criminologists often tap a variety of theoretical perspectives across disciplines at various levels of analysis (e.g., individual level, macro level) in order to better explain the complexities of and response to delinquency and crime, as well as other associated deviant behaviors. In this section, psychopathy, an individual level, psychological construct (personality disorder), will be discussed along with other more traditionally recognized criminological correlates, which are not always familiar in form and presentation to other disciplines, such as psychology.

Though the relationship between the clinically recognized construct of psychopathy and anti-social behavior is well recognized in the psychological literature, attempts are being made to merge these findings with criminological research to enhance understanding (e.g., Vaughn, Howard, & DeLisi, 2008). DeLisi (2009), in particular, suggests that criminologists acknowledge the robust findings associated with psychopathy and career criminality compared to that of one of the leading criminological theories, Gottfredson and Hirschi's (1990) a general theory of crime (GTC), frequently referred to as self-control theory (DeLisi, 2009; see also Pratt & Cullen, 2000). In his article, DeLisi further gives attention to significant research identifying the importance of psychopathy as a robust predictor of explicitly career criminality. Yet, as with other known correlates of delinquency, with the recognition that psychopathic traits are normally distributed in the population of youth, it is important to further evaluate this association in nonconfined samples while incorporating what is known about problematic adolescent behavior. At the clinical and subclinical level, it is important to appreciate how these traits (or states) behave amid other known predictors of delinquency.

This attention to psychopathy in criminological literature is not new. Psychopathy tends to cycle in and out of consideration as criminologists have long debated the usefulness of psychopathy in studying criminality.

Travis Hirschi (1969, p. 17), for instance, offered the following:

> *In explaining deviant behavior, psychologists, in con-*
> *trast, emphasize insensitivity to the opinion of others. Unfor-*
> *tunately, they too tend to ignore variation, and, in addition,*
> *they tend to tie sensitivity inextricably to other variables, to*
> *make it part of a syndrome or "type," and thus seriously to*
> *reduce its value as an explanatory concept. The psychopath is*
> *characterized only in part by "deficient attachment to or af-*
> *fection for others, a failure to respond to the ordinary motiva-*
> *tions founded in respect or regard for one's fellows"; he is*
> *also characterized by such things as "excessive aggressive-*
> *ness," "lack of superego control," and "an infantile level of*
> *response." Unfortunately, too, the behavior that psychopathy*
> *is used to explain often becomes part of the definition of psy-*
> *chopathy.*

Hirschi emphasized concern for the circular process of using anti-social behavior to infer mental abnormality while using the mental abnormality to explain anti-social behavior (here he quotes Wootton, 1959). He further argued that, "The problems of diagnosis, tautology, and name-calling are avoided if the dimensions of psychopathy are treated as causally and therefore problematically interrelated, rather than as logically and therefore necessarily bound to each other. In fact, it can be argued that all the characteristics attributed to the psychopath follow from, are effects of, his lack of attachment to others" (Hirschi, 1969, p. 17).

Of course, Hirschi offers more to his reasoning and concerns, but several of the points he is making can be used to inform our purposes here. First, criminologists have periodically tapped and considered the construct of psychopathy to inform discussions and theory. In the name of progress, real attention needs to be paid to the definition and measurement issues that were identified in the past and persist today. Second, by extension, there is a reasonable argument to be made about separating the features of psychopathy for study and consider these features and manifestations as causally linked. For example, do similar processes promote or cause callousness and impulsivity? Does callousness contribute to impulsivity? Of course, Hirschi explains psychopathy and everything attributable to them as stemming from a lack of attachment to others (bonding). In that way, a psychopath is one who has no effectual bonds and therefore no moral constraints and behavior flows from that reality. Hence, Hirschi makes another striking claim about psychopathy that is worth noting, "lack of attachment to others is not merely a symptom of psychopathy, it is psychopathy; lack of conscience is just another way of saying the same thing, and the violation of norms is (or may be) a consequence" (1969, p. 18). One can readily infer that he intends to account for psychopathy in his social bonding theory.

Contemporary Efforts to Incorporate Psychopathy

The concept of psychopathy has been furnished as an explanation for criminal career trajectories because of the reasonable stability and prevalence of psychopathic features among high frequency offenders (e.g., Vaughn & DeLisi, 2008). Though psychopathy is traditionally conceived as a psychiatric/personality disorder, as opposed to fitting into the framework of criminological theory, psychopathic individuals share several notable characteristics, which have been touched upon earlier, including being callous, self-centered, interpersonally exploitive, socially inappropriate in attempts to satisfy needs, deficient in being able to secure affectional bonds with others, among other characteristics (Vaughn & Howard, 2005, p. 236). Though scholars are recognizing the promise of incorporating psychopathic characteristics into the study of delinquency and crime in criminology (Vaughn, Howard, & DeLisi, 2008), these studies most often are limited to predicting career offending (e.g., DeLisi, 2009; Salekin, 2008; Vaughn & DeLisi, 2008; Weibe, 2003) and may be confounded by the contamination problems associated with the psychopathy construct. Further, very few studies have examined psychopathy alongside other consistent and traditional correlates of adolescent delinquency in non-institutionalized populations, though this is changing (see e.g., Flexon & Meldrum, 2013; Vaughn, Litschge, DeLisi, Beaver, & McMillen, 2008).

As already discussed, scholars are appreciating that the collective characteristics that make up the construct of psychopathy are largely normally distributed in the population (DeLisi, 2009; Edens, Marcus, & Vaughn, 2011; Murrie et al., 2007). This is valuable for discerning which features are more or less associated with problematic outcomes depending on whether an individual is in the general or confined populations and if an individual can be described as more or less psychopathic.

It is important to recognize that certain characteristics of psychopathy may be differentially important to the study of general delinquency. Previously reviewed was that the characteristics housed under Factor 2 of the PCL-R, the Social Deviance Scale, better predict antisocial outcomes, for obvious reasons. An impressive amount of research has demonstrated that the behavioral features used to measure psychopathy underlie the association between psychopathy and antisocial/ criminal-type behaviors (Hawes et al., 2014, p. 631).

Things are more nuanced when it comes to the more affective dimensions of psychopathy or those that would fall under Factor 1, the interpersonal/affective domain of Hare's PCL measures, which again is considered the gold standard. Though the study of psychopathic traits in criminal populations has often focused on examining criminal

FLEXON

trajectories among serious, chronic offenders, far less is known about the value of these qualities in predicting delinquency in the general population of youth. In addition, little is known about how certain non-behavior psychopathic traits may interact with criminological constructs to increase or diminish the probability of delinquency.

Some of these criminological constructs can actually be conceived of as indicators of psychopathy, such as with impulsivity/low self-control and poor bonding. Protective and vulnerability factors known to affect psychopathology symptoms have been taken for granted in other disciplines (e.g., Muris, Mayer, Reinders, & Wesenhagen, 2011). It is reasonable to assume other individual-level characteristics in the presence of psychopathic symptoms might mollify or exacerbate the effects of psychopathic traits on juvenile anti-social behavior. For instance, might possessing high levels of CU psychopathic traits necessarily result in anti-social behavior? Some research suggests that it is not enough in and of itself (e.g., Flexon, 2015, 2016).

For review, youth high in CU traits fitting the profile of the primary variant showed associated anti-social behavior in the presence of problem, neglectful parenting. Here, is the youth's response to the parenting the causative feature for anti-social behavior? Does an inability to effectively monitor such youth via poor parenting practices result in them associating with deviant peers and then delinquency (Kimonis et al., 2004)? Did this youth learn a problematic behavioral repertoire similar to their parents, or is their behavior a reaction to it? Does the youth suffer from insecure (e.g., avoidant, disorganized) attachment and are they dissociating, which would look like CU traits? This also alerts to the idea that we may have a blind spot when it comes to psychopathy as previously discussed. Essentially, we may know more about those deemed psychopathic because their problem behavior draws attention from authorities. These youths are likely identified as psychopathic during their juvenile or criminal justice intake or other type of mandatory assessment owning, in part, to their behavior.

Traditional Delinquency Correlates

While research provides evidence of the importance of psychopathy as a predictor of delinquent and violent behavior, what has been inadequately addressed is the relative influence of psychopathic traits on delinquent behavior in conjunction with other key, more traditionally researched criminological variables. Moreover, the recognition that moderation may occur in the presence of additional risk factors has long been observed in the criminological research, prompting further theoretical development and empirical understanding. As recognized by Hay and colleagues (2006), ''... cooccurring causes of crime likely amplify the effects of one another'' (p. 328).

Several variables from within the criminological literature have emerged as consistent predictors of juvenile delinquency and violent behavior, in particular. Though hardly exhaustive, the following will highlight several of the more prominent. Among them, the role of school bonding is frequently seen in delinquency theory and research, as the relationship is a central premise of control theories of delinquency (e.g., Hirschi, 1969). For illustration, in relying on traditional control theory, Thornberry (1987, p. 866) describes its relevance in his presentation of interactional theory. Here, commitment to school is seen as symbolic of a youth's conformity to prosocial activities and convention and ''represents the granting of legitimacy to such middle-class

values as education, personal industry, financial success, deferral of gratification, and the like.'' Thus, when commitment to school is high, delinquency is low as an artifact of effective social bonding to one of the most important socializing agents of youth. Research has repeatedly evinced this association (e.g., Cernkovich & Giordano, 1992; Kelly & Pink, 1973; Thornberry, Lizotte, Krohn, Farnworth, & Joon Jang, 1991). School bonding also is implicated with psychopathy. It seems clear that those having issues with CU traits and other manifestations of psychopathy may have problems establishing bonds to school. Because of this, research that disaggregates and evaluates characteristics and traits independently offers clues as to which features are more implicated with behavioral outcomes.

In addition, the link between inept parenting practices and delinquency has one of the longest empirical histories in criminological re-

search. Since the late 1930s, the work of Sheldon and Eleanor Glueck highlighted a number of factors associated with delinquents, chief among them was the role of ineffective parenting (Glueck & Glueck, 1950). In fact, the prevailing theory in criminology, the general theory of crime (GTC), builds upon these findings. The balance of current research continues to show that ineffective parenting including the lack of effective monitoring, supervision, and discipline, as well as parental rejection place youth at risk for delinquency (for a meta-analysis of 161 studies on parenting and delinquency research, see Hoeve et al., 2009).

Self-control is also one of the most studied correlates of delinquency in criminology following the advent of Gottfredson and Hirschi's (1990) work. In the GTC, the failure of self-control to develop in a youth by age 10 as a result of ineffective parenting is postulated to explain the balance of crime and delinquency. In extensive reviews of the research on self-control, Pratt and Cullen (2000) and de Ridder, Lensvelt-Mulders, Finkenauer, Stok, and Baumeister (2012) report that self-control has a consistent, but modest relationship with delinquency across a variety of studies. Different disciplines recognize the concept of self-control. Such constructs, which are similarly named, deal with self-regulation, such as self-control or perceived control as used in psychology which, like Gottfredson and Hirschi's construct, also involve behavior regulation (Weisz & Stipek, 1982). In kind, the impulsivity dimension (Factor 2) of psychopathy also mirrors this notion of self-regulation, or specifically, the lack of self-regulation (impulsivity). Such widespread recognition of the self-control construct across disciplines is meaningful. Since the CU dimension, which excludes impulsivity, seems most implicated in identifying juvenile psychopathy in the literature, adding this construct of impulsivity/low self-control separately as its own entity is warranted. Further, correlational analysis supports the notion that the CU dimension (part of Factor 1) and impulsivity as a feature of low self-control and having aspects of psychopathy (a portion of Factor 2) are measuring different things (r. 20; Flexon & Meldrum, 2013).

Frequently studied in tandem with low self-control is the influence of peer delinquency on youth crime. Delinquent peer affiliation is perhaps one of the most robust correlates of delinquency studied in criminology, withstanding scrutiny when tested among other germane delinquency correlates

(see Akers & Jensen, 2006; Pratt et al., 2010). Delinquent peer association is linked with a myriad of delinquent behaviors including violence. Hence, the body of research implicates the above correlates as important in the etiology of adolescent anti-social behaviors.

Other criminological correlates have been noted in earlier chapters and are highlighted by the OJJDP, which are encompassed by various traditions in the criminological literature, e.g., strain theory, control and social bonding theories, social learning theory, social conflict theory, social disorganization theory, etcetera. Certain characteristics, such as race, ethnicity, and sex are also consistent predictors holding a place in the criminological literature.

Given the research providing strong evidence that psychopathic CU traits, in addition to variables considered to be central to theories of delinquency, predict a wide range of adolescent anti-social behavior, an important consideration that has not received much attention is how these common correlates operate to explain delinquency when accounting for CU traits. The failure to consider whether key criminological variables continue to predict anti-social juvenile behavior amidst psychopathic traits runs the risk of model misspecification. While it is possible that psychopathic traits explain a degree of the variation seen in violent and anti-social juvenile behavior traditionally accounted for by other correlates of delinquency, this possibility has yet to receive adequate attention in the literature.

Also needing consideration is whether and to what extent psychopathic traits might interact with such constructs to the extent that they remain robust predictors of delinquency after accounting for psychopathic traits. While conventional understanding and research shows that there

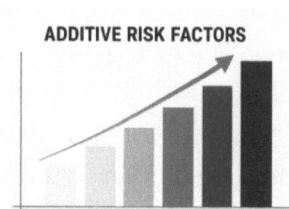

ADDITIVE RISK FACTORS

are additive effects of risk factors, i.e., more risk factors increase the likelihood of poor outcomes, few studies have addressed the issue of amplification directly (but see DeLisi et al., 2018; Flexon & Meldrum, 2013). In considering how such interactions might manifest themselves, different outcomes are possible. One result is guided by the principle that in the presence of multiple causes of crime, there will be an amplification effect on negative behavioral outcomes. This understanding is borrowed from prominent criminological theories, such as general strain theory and social bonding theory, as well as research (see e.g., Hay, Fortson, Hollist, Altheimer, & Schaible, 2006). It is plausible that the presence of psychopathic CU traits and other risk factors for violence (e.g., low self-control and frequent delinquent peer affiliation) could result in an amplification effect. For example, an individual possessing strong psychopathic traits might be more likely to engage in violence in the presence of delinquent peers as opposed to an individual who associates with delinquent peers but lacks psychopathic traits.

For example, Kimonis, Frick, and Barry (2004) evaluated whether delinquent peer association differed between anti-social youth with and without CU traits. Their findings suggested that youth having a CU interpersonal style have the greatest level of delinquent peer involvement (p. 263). It was suggestive that amplification in delinquency may result from this association. Beyond this and the few studies noted, however, there appears to be a paucity of research considering the conditional nature of psychopathic traits, and in particular the CU dimension, and germane criminological variables to predict delinquency. As such, the possibilities discussed above require future evaluation.

In observation of DeLisi's (2009) argument, the emergence of psychopathy or more specifically, the psychopathic traits of callousness, unemotionality, and remorselessness, as predictors of adolescent anti-social behavior were evaluated in a study conducted by Flexon and Meldrum (2013). Importantly, a nonconfined sample of youth was appraised, and the findings of the study showed several things. Among the correlates of juvenile anti-sociality evaluated, only peer violence had a stronger correlation than the psychopathic features of callousness, unemotionality, and remorselessness (CU traits) combined. Additionally, CU traits were important predictors of violent juvenile behavior among the general population of youth alongside other predictors of delinquency. These traits demonstrated a relatively clear association with violent youth behavior that was comparable or stronger than many other known correlates of delinquency. At the same time, it is of equal importance to note that, in large part, the traditional criminological correlates of delinquency maintained significance alongside CU traits, speaking to the well-established finding that no one single variable explains all of delinquency, and that a number of risk factors can be contributing to behavioral outcomes.

Conditional effects also were observed in their analysis for violent peer association and CU traits, as well as low self-control and CU traits. The interactions suggested complimentary possibilities. Based on their findings, it appears that in the presence of high CU, the effects of having low self-control or affiliating with violent peers is diminished. The alternatives are also true. The findings suggest that when one characteristic is prevailing to the other risk factors in the same individual, the dominant characteristic has the greatest influence on violent delinquency. In other words, some of these major risk factors, namely CU traits, low self-control, and delinquent peer affiliation, are somewhat interchangeable or transposable for one another. Hence, their findings suggest that violence increases in the presence of one risk factor (e.g., CU traits, low self-control, or delinquent peers), but the addition of other risk factors increases violence only by diminishing margins.

Problematically, the construct of psychopathy used in the study was treated as a unified measure. That is, no attention was paid to disaggregating youth according to whether they were primary or secondary. This is a limitation for reasons already discussed in previous chapters. It also must be recognized that there may be mediation among the variables used in the study. Though evaluating this was beyond the intent of their research, future efforts would do well to evaluate this possibility.

Directions for Future Research

Several directions and improvements for further research are suggested by the above discussion. Consistent are findings showing psychopathy is connected to anti-sociality. However, there is a lot of tension among scholars concerning measurement and this outcome. There is concern that there is no consistent definition of psychopathy (while even saying that can be like stepping on a landmine), and as a result, there is heterogeneity across findings. While there are a number of studies vetting the different measures against one another, this seems to further alert to the idea that disagreement concerning the essential features of psychopathy still exists.

Future research should seek to evaluate the different proffered dimensions of psychopathy (i.e., narcissism, dishonest charm, grandiosity, lying, etcetera) separately and alongside traditional criminological delinquency correlates to determine the value of other dimensions of psychopathy to general delinquency and anti-sociality and, as such, criminological thought. This research should also seek to evaluate the presence of time order among these different characteristics by employing a longitudinal design to further evaluate of the role of psychopathic CU traits among the other traditional delinquency correlates toward understanding juvenile anti-social behavior. Studies are suggestive of such dynamics.

Instructive is research establishing that psychopathic traits may influence the presence of self-control. In recent work, Vaughn and colleagues (2007) incorporated psychopathology and self-control in their study of 723 youth confined under the supervision of the Missouri Division of Youth Services. The purpose of their study was to assess the value of using mental health, psychopathic, and substance abuse variables to predict self-control (p. 809). The researchers found a significant connection between psychopathy and self-control, and, in particular, their research demonstrates the consequence of the psychopathic feature of narcissism in driving low self-control. Their study illustrates the interplay between these significant constructs as delinquency precursors, as well as highlighting the import of considering numerous individual level characteristics in the study of problematic behaviors.

Of note, DeLisi and colleagues (2018) recent work also vetted psychopathy alongside low self-control in models examining varied anti-social outcomes and victimization. Their psychopathy measure was a modified version of the Psychopathic Personality Inventory short form (PPI; Lilienfeld & Andrews, 1996; short-form variant is the PPI-SF; Lilienfeld & Hess, 2001), which importantly excludes behavioral items. The measure was not disaggregated by subtypes of psychopaths, however. The purpose of the study was to compare the virtues of psychopathy and self-control as general criminological theories. Low self-control was the dominant theory for explanatory power with results indicating that low self-control predicted violent offending, property offending, self-reported delinquency and victimization, whereas psychopathy was associated with property offending, self-reported delinquency and intermittently with victimization. Readers are encouraged to consult DeLisi et al., (2018) for more nuanced findings, but the results led to the conclusion that, "In terms of engaging in pathological forms of delinquency, extreme deficits in self-control are more predictive than extreme psychopathy scores" (2018, p. 67). Of note, other covariates alongside psychopathy and low self-control remained predictive of anti-social outcomes, such as race, ethnicity, age and prior drug use. In fact, race was the most powerful of all study variables in predicting violence, delinquency and victimization and prior year drug use had the largest effect on property offending. Other common significant controls, such as delinquent peers and other drivers were not included in the study. However, this and others' recent work is moving the bar toward integrating psychopathy into the criminological literature. More work is clearly needed, and it appears that there is real interest in developing this area.

Toward Further Advancing Theory:

The Clustering of Psychopathy in Place and Race

Evidence suggests that neighborhood context might influence the effects of psychopathic traits on behavior (Meier, Slutske, Arndt, & Cadoret, 2008). Meier and colleagues (2008) findings suggest that various contextual features attributable to neighborhood environments influence the association between psychopathy and behavior. The association between impulsive CU traits and delinquency was stronger in at risk neighborhoods. This is suggestive of a couple of possibilities. One notion is that there could be genetic clustering. This idea carries with it a profound concern connected to the debate over a *crime gene* or *warrior gene* (for discussion see Gillett & Tamatea, 2012). Alternatively, it could be that characteristics of certain neighborhoods are drivers of individual states that are associated with anti-social behavior. The idea that some places are criminogenic is hardly new, e.g., social disorganization theory. It also could be attributed to anti-social friendship networks, e.g., contagion and social learning theory, which tend to be associated with clustering in certain locations. On this point, recent work has indicated that susceptibility to peer pressure differs by variant type (Fanti et al., 2013; Flexon, 2015). If there are differentially more psychopathic variants clustered in certain locations owning to a concentration of environmental drivers, then further negative influence may be realized through association with other troubled youth. Strain theory could also be attached to such findings. Hence, future efforts should take the impact of neighborhood risk factors and variation into account because it could be that environmental features drive forces that influence psychopathy, self-control, other vulnerabilities and anti-sociality.

In actuality, the notion that environmental features may influence the prevalence and incidence of psychopathy is reasonable as such relationships are likely complex. One issue is that it is difficult to sort out what is happening in the aggregate. We know that some youth tend to grow out of their labelled psychopathy or psychopathic-like states, low self-control and anti-social behavior and other characteristics attributable to adolescent development. The mechanisms owning to a particular location that underlie continuity or lack of stability may be different depending upon the individual. These things are lost in much research examining statistical associations in the aggregate. It is not to say that such research is not useful. It certainly is but it becomes difficult to disentangle the factors relevant to specific individuals owning to particular locations.

Contention also surrounds whether psychopathy clusters by race. Since race is a very stable and consistent correlate of crime (research on this point is ubiquitous), scholars have cautioned that there may be an overrepresentation of minorities labelled as psychopathic owning to measurement and risk assessment tools. Some research demonstrates racial clustering such that black adults are more likely to meet psychopathy criteria and score higher on PCL measures than white adults; Researchers also found distinctions in the factor structure such that impulsivity mattered more for discerning psychopathy for whites than for blacks (Kosson Smith, & Newman, 1990). However, others report finding the opposite. In reporting their findings, Vachon and colleagues (2012) assert that, "Moderation effects for race and criminal status were rare, occurring at a rate (5.7%) approximating chance (5%); when significant, the effects were trivial in magnitude" (p. 266, 268).

Despite the examples noted above, questions remain concerning whether current measures are equally useful across offenders of different racial or ethnic backgrounds. Research devoted to the generalizability of instruments across race and ethnicity for adult samples is more available than for youth (for discussion see Seagrave & Grisso, 2002). In fact, the inconsistency in the research that has been done on youth lead some to conclude that, "these results raise "red flags" regarding relations between ethnicity and measures of psychopathic traits in children and adolescents. More research in this area is required to confidently rule out that item, method, or construct bias are not present in juvenile psychopathy instruments, particularly because developmental research suggests that "normal" minority adolescents experience greater obstacles in identity development" (Seagrave & Grisso, 2002, p. 237). Yet again, questions are not settled.

Another thing to consider along this line is that while minorities are overrepresented in the criminal justice system given their representation in the population, they are also well represented in at risk neighborhoods. This is for various reasons, e.g., poverty/social conflict explanations. Obviously, how these factors and or drivers relate with psychopathy is worthy of further investigation. The development of an interactional theory with regard to psychopathy may be useful, e.g., Thornberry, (1987).

The Role of CU Traits, Punishment Responses and Cognition in Advancing Theory

Research demonstrates a degree of impairment among some with high CU traits, which points to poor processing of fear and deficits in learning as a result of punishment insensitivity (Frick & Ray, 2015). According to Frick and Ray (2015), this has implications for conscience development, for which lack of empathy and guilt are key features of CU traits. Clearly, there are implications for developmental theories of psychopathy, which in turn informs treatment. The presence of guilt and empathy help shape prosocial emotions and behavior, and the lack thereof likely contributes to the opposite.

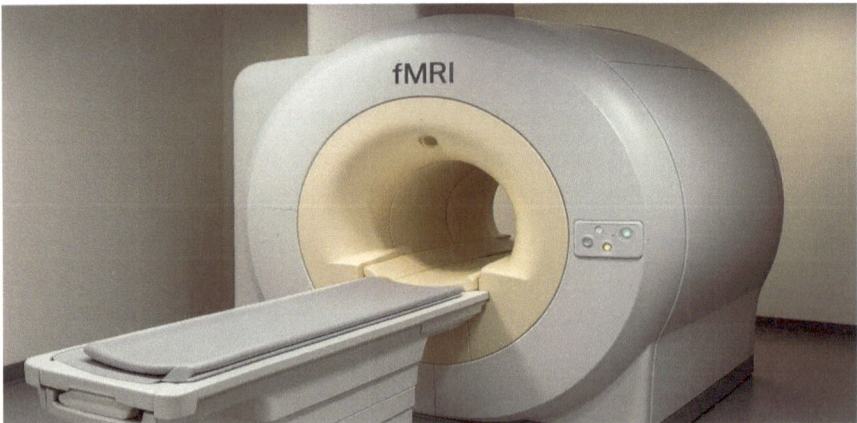

Other research examining distinctions between successful psychopaths (not criminally involved) and unsuccessful psychopaths (criminally involved) (Cleckley, 1941, 1948) has noted that since psychopaths can be found in all walks of life, generalizations based on forensic samples should be avoided. With that understanding, Gao and Raine (2010) hypothesize that among psychopaths able to avoid criminality, or at least being caught up in the criminal justice system, the distinction with forensic samples lies in differences with intact or enhanced neurobiological processing among those deemed successful psychopaths.

These unimpaired processes include better executive functioning, heightened skin conductance reactivity, and normative volumes and functioning of the prefrontal cortex and amygdala (p. 194). According to the researchers, deficits in these same areas among criminal psychopaths may be predisposing them to more extreme forms of anti-social behavior or render them less likely to pick up on cues of future punishment. However, the evidence finding differences in a number of these areas is still lacking, inconsistent or finds no differences in populations of psychopaths.

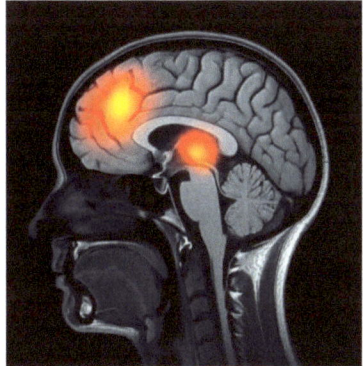

A barrier to studies examining the brain function between criminal and non-criminal psychopaths is how these groups are defined. Of the studies that have been conducted, various strategies and inclusion criteria have been used to capture psychopathic groups included in the studies. Without being able to come to uniform definitions and inclusion criteria for psychopathy, successful psychopathy and unsuccessful psychopathy or primary and secondary, this area of research will continue to be plagued with issues of reliability. Hence, the same hindrances to psychopathy research in general plague study focusing on the nuances of the disorder. It is a given that more research is needed, and this area needs further refinement and development. However, the emergence of consistent, reliable findings would be informative to current theoretical orientations of psychopathy.

The Future of Treatments? Epigenetics and Psychopathy

An area of emerging interest is in epigenetics. Epigenetics, very simply, refers to the interaction of certain factors—such as environment—and genetic expression, whereby changes in people (or organisms) are the result of DNA and histone modification. These modifications can lead to the heritable silencing or activation of genes (phenotype) without altering the genetic code itself (DNA gene sequence; genotype; Egger, Liang, Aparicio, & Jones, 2004, p. 457). In other words, epigenetic processes influence *if* and *when* genes are expressed. These changes may result from environmental or personal influences, such as prenatal and postnatal exposures, nutritional status, and chronic stressors and can ultimately contribute to both physical and mental illness (e.g., Egger et al., 2004; Heijmans et al., 2008; Jirtle & Skinner, 2007; Painter, Roseboom, & Bleker, 2005; van Os & Selten, 1998).

A growing body of research shows that Adverse Childhood Experiences (ACEs), including abuse, neglect, and household dysfunction, can act as potent environmental stressors that shape the developing brain. Chronic activation of the stress response system in early life can alter epigenetic regulation of neural and hormonal pathways, leading to enduring changes in emotional processing, impulse control, and stress reactivity. In the context of psychopathy, this is especially relevant: while primary psychopathy is more strongly associated with innate temperamental traits and low fear reactivity, secondary psychopathy is consistently linked to early-life trauma and environmental adversity. These traumatic exposures do not simply create "bad experiences" in a social sense—they can leave molecular marks on the genome, modifying the expression of genes involved in emotional regulation, empathy, and aggression.

Since genetics have been implicated in the etiology of psychopathy, it is unsurprising that the study of epigenetics has quickly entered the conversation. This research is still in its infancy but connects neatly with work on the neurobiological underpinnings of the disorder. For example, trauma-related epigenetic modifications may disrupt the development of prefrontal and limbic circuitry, compounding behavioral risk in youth predisposed to callous–unemotional traits. Recognizing this interplay opens the door to targeted interventions—ones that address not only the behavioral manifestations of psychopathy but also the biological embedding of early adversity.

Egger and colleagues (2004) highlight the hope for the development of new epigenetic therapies for disease. Lessons learned from other conditions, such as cancer, suggest that modifying epigenetic marks could one day alter maladaptive patterns of gene expression. In theory, such approaches could mitigate the enduring impact of ACE-related trauma on neurodevelopment, potentially reducing the severity of secondary psychopathy. While the idea of using epigenetic interventions for a personality disorder raises ethical and legal questions (for discussion, see Tamatea, 2015), the integration of genetic, environmental, and neurobiological knowledge represents a promising frontier in the search for effective treatments.

The Bottom Line

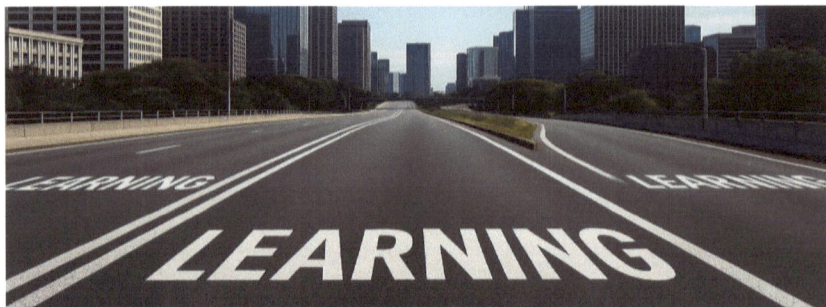

On a final note, irrespective of the controversies and challenges noted throughout this work, one theme remains constant: there is a persistent desire to find answers. Thoughtful and dedicated scholars from a variety of fields, including psychology, neuroscience, criminology, and related, continue to press forward, aware of both the promise and the pitfalls inherent in studying psychopathy in youth. While genuine progress has been made, there is also recognition that the complexity of developmental psychopathy resists simple solutions.

The paradox is striking: despite decades of research spanning multiple disciplines and theoretical perspectives, we are often left with more questions than answers. Yet this should not be mistaken for a void of knowledge. On the contrary, the accumulation of findings—on genetics, neurobiology, trauma, epigenetics, and social context—demonstrates that nascent psychopathy is neither a mystery nor a monolith. Instead, it is a field marked by nuance, competing explanations, and the urgent need for integration across perspectives.

What this ultimately signals is not failure but opportunity. The recognition that so much remains unresolved underscores the importance of continued inquiry, especially inquiry that bridges disciplines and translates into effective, ethical interventions. If the study of juvenile psychopathy teaches us anything, it is that early behavior cannot be reduced to inevitability. Rather, it should motivate a deeper commitment to understanding the interplay between biology, environment, and experience—so that treatment, prevention, and policy responses are informed by both humility and hope.

CHAPTER 6 MAIN POINTS

❖ While a connection between psychopathy and anti-social behavior is well recognized in the psychological literature, recent attempts are being made to merge these findings with criminological research.

❖ Criminologists have long debated the usefulness of psychopathy in studying criminality.

❖ Hirschi emphasized concern for the circular process of using anti-social behavior to infer psychopathy while using psychopathy to explain anti-social behavior.

❖ Traditionally recognized criminological correlates include constructs from various disciplines, e.g., low self-control (impulsivity), delinquent peers, poor social bonding or social control, social disorganization and neighborhood context, race.

❖ Research indicates that in models examining anti-social outcomes, CU traits do not exhaust the explanatory power of other criminological correlates.

❖ Future research should exploit findings that psychopathy can cluster, replicate such findings, and discern explanations consistent with those findings.

❖ Research examining biological differences and impairments in criminal psychopaths, as well as epigenetics deserves further development and refinement.

REFERENCES

Almas, I., & Lordos, A. (2025). A narrative review of psychopathy research: Current advances and the argument for a qualitative approach. *The Journal of Forensic Psychiatry & Psychology, 36*(3), 356–406. https://doi.org/10.1080/14789949.2025.2456208

Andershed, H., Kerr, M., Stattin, H., & Levander, S. (2002). Psychopathic traits in non-referred youths: A new assessment tool. In E. Blauuw and L. Sheridan (Eds.), *Psychopaths: Current international perspectives* (pp. 131-158). The Hague: Elsevier.

Andrews DA & Bonta J. (1995). *LSI-R: the level of service inventory-revised.* Multi-Health Systems.

Akers, R. L., & Jensen, G. F. (2006). The empirical status of social learning theory of crime and deviance: The past, present, and future. In F. T. Cullen, J. P. Wright, & K. R. Blevins (Eds.), *Taking stock: The status of criminological theory* (pp. 37–76). New Brunswick, NJ: Transaction.

Argueta-Cevallos, G. (2021). A prosecutor with a smoking gun: Examining the weaponization of race, psychopathy, and ASPD labels in capital cases. *Colum. Hum. Rts. L. Rev., 53,* 624-662.

Aspinwall, L. G., Brown, T. R., & Tabery, J. (2012). The double-edged sword: Does biomechanism increase or decrease judges' sentencing of psychopaths? *Science, 337*(6096), 846-849.

Astridge, B., Li, W. W., McDermott, B., & Longhitano, C. (2023). A systematic review and meta-analysis on adverse childhood experiences: Prevalence in youth offenders and their effects on youth recidivism. *Child Abuse & Neglect, 140,* 106055, ISSN 0145-2134, https://doi.org/10.1016/j.chiabu.2023.106055

https://www.sciencedirect.com/science/article/pii/S014521342300036
4

Balia, C., Carucci, S., Coghill, D., & Zuddas, A. (2018). The pharma-cological treatment of aggression in children and adolescents with conduct disorder. Do callous-unemotional traits modulate the efficacy of medication?. *Neuroscience and biobehavioral reviews*, *91*, 218–238. https://doi.org/10.1016/j.neubiorev.2017.01.024

Barry, C. T., Frick, P. J., DeShazo, T. M., McCoy, M. G., Ellis, M., & Loney, B. R. (2000). The importance of callous-unemotional traits for extending the concept of psychopathy to children. *Journal of Abnor-mal Psychology*, *109*, 335–340.

Baskin-Sommers, A. R., Curtin, J. J., & Newman, J. P. (2015). Alter-ing the cognitive-affective dysfunctions of psychopathic and external-izing offender subtypes with cognitive remediation. *Clinical Psycho-logical Science*, *3*(1), 45-57.

Beaver, K. M., Boutwell, B. B., Barnes, J. C., Vaughn, M. G., & DeL-isi, M. (2015). The association between psychopathic personality traits and criminal justice outcomes: Results from a nationally representative sample of males and females. *Crime & Delinquency, 63(6),* 708-730.

Beaver, K. M., Hartman, S., & Belsky, J. (2015). Differential suscepti-bility to parental sensitivity based on early-life temperament in the prediction of adolescent affective psychopathic personality traits. *Criminal Justice and Behavior, 42*(5), 546-565.

Bezdjian, S., Raine, A., Baker, L. A., & Lynam, D. R. (2011). Psycho-pathic personality in children: Genetic and environmental contribu-tions. *Psychological Medicine, 41*, 589–600.

Blais, J., Solodukhin, E., & Forth, A. E. (2014). A meta-analysis exploring the relationship between psychopathy and instrumental versus reactive violence. *Criminal Justice and Behavior, 41*, 797–821.

Boer, D.P., Hart, S.D., Kropp, P.R., & Webster, C.D. (1997). *Manual for the sexual violence risk-20. Professional guidelines for assessing risk of sexual violence.* Simon Fraser University, Mental Health, Law, and Policy Institute.

Boonmann, C., Pérez, T., Schmid, M., Fegert, J., Jauk, E., & Schmeck, K. (2020). Psychometric properties of the German version of the Youth Psychopathic Traits Inventory–Short Version (YPI-S). *BMC Psychiatry, 20,* 548. https://doi.org/10.1186/s12888-020-02943-z

Borum, R., Bartel, P., & Forth, A. (2002). *Manual for the structured assessment of violence risk in youth (SAVRY).* University of South Florida.

Borum, R., Bartel, P., & Forth, A. (2003). *Manual for the structured assessment of violence risk in youth (SAVRY): version 1.1.* University of South Florida.

Brown, D., Larkin, F., Sengupta, S., Romero-Ureclay, J. L., Ross, C. C., Gupta, N., Vinestock, M., & Das, M. (2014). Clozapine: an effective treatment for seriously violent and psychopathic men with antisocial personality disorder in a UK high-security hospital. *CNS Spectrums, 19*(5), 391-402.

Camp, J. P., Skeem, J. L., Barchard, K., Lilienfeld, S. O., & Poythress, N. G. (2013). Psychopathic predators? Getting specific about the relation between psychopathy and violence. *Journal of Consulting and Clinical Psychology, 81*, 467–480.

Cauffman, E., Skeem, J., Dmitrieva, J., & Cavanagh, C. (2016). Comparing the stability of psychopathy scores in adolescents versus adults:

How often is "fledgling psychopathy" misdiagnosed? *Psychology, Public Policy, and Law, 22*(1), 77-91.

Cernkovich, S. A., & Giordano, P. C. (1992). School bonding, race, and delinquency. *Criminology, 30*, 261–291.

Cleckley, H. (1941, 1976, 5th). *The mask of sanity.* St. Louis, MO; C.V. Mosby.

Coelho, C. M., Araújo, A. S., Suttiwan, P., Barbosa, F., Bento, T., & Zsido, A. N. (2025). Psychopathy: What are fearless people afraid of? *Frontiers in Psychiatry, 16,* 1574813. https://doi.org/10.3389/fpsyt.2025.1574813

Conger, R.D., & Elder, G.H. (1994). *Families in troubled times: Adapting to change in rural America.* New York: Aldine de Gruyter.

Cooke, D. J., Hart, S. D., Logan, C., & Michie, C. (2004). *Comprehensive Assessment of Psychopathic Personality – Institutional Rating Scale (CAPP-IRS).* Glasgow, UK: Department of Psychology, Glasgow Caledonian University.

Cooke, D. J., Hart, S. D., Logan, C., & Michie, C. (2012). Explicating the construct of psychopathy: Development and validation of a conceptual model, the Comprehensive Assessment of Psychopathic Personality (CAPP). *International Journal of Forensic Mental Health, 11*(4), 242-252.

Cooke, D. J., & Michie, C. (2001). Refining the construct of psychopathy: Toward a hierarchical model. *Psychological Assessment, 13*, 171–188.

Dadds, M. R., Moul, C., Cauchi, A., Dobson-Stone, C., Hawes, D. J., Brennan, J., & Ebstein, R. E. (2014). Methylation of the oxytocin receptor gene and oxytocin blood levels in the development of psychopathy. *Development and Psychopathology, 26*(1), 33-40.

da Silva, D. R., Rijo, D., & Salekin, R. T. (2012). Child and adolescent psychopathy: A state-of-the-art reflection on the construct and etiological theories. *Journal of Criminal Justice, 40*(4), 269-277.

Dawson, S., McCuish, E., Hart, S. D., & Corrado, R. R. (2012). Critical issues in the assessment of adolescent psychopathy: An illustration using two case studies. *International Journal of Forensic Mental Health, 11*(2), 63-79.

DeLisi, M. (2009). Psychopathy is the unified theory of crime. *Youth Violence and Juvenile Justice, 7*, 256–273.

DeLisi, M., Tostlebe, J., Burgason, K., Heirigs, M., & Vaughn, M. (2018). Self-control versus psychopathy: A head-to-head test of general theories of antisociality. *Youth Violence and Juvenile Justice, 16*(1), 53-76.

DeMatteo, D., & Olver, M. E. (2022). Use of the Psychopathy Checklist-Revised in legal contexts: Validity, reliability, admissibility, and evidentiary issues. *Journal of Personality Assessment, 104*(2), 234-251. https://doi.org/10.1080/00223891.2021.1955693

de Ridder, D. T. D., Lensvelt-Mulders, G., Finkenauer, C., Stok, F. M., & Baumeister, R. F. (2012). Taking stock of self-control: A meta-analysis of how trait self-control relates to a wide range of behaviors. *Personality and Social Psychology Review, 16*, 76–99.

Development Services Group, Inc. (2015). *Risk Factors for Delinquency. Literature review.* Office of Juvenile Justice and Delinquency Prevention. Washington, D.C.: Available online at https://www.ojjdp.gov/mpg/litreviews/Risk%20Factors.pdf. Prepared by Development Services Group, Inc., under cooperative agreement number 2013–JF–FX–K002.

Dolan, M. (2004). Psychopathic personality in young people. *Advances in Psychiatric Treatment, 10*(6), 466-473.

Donohue, M. R., Hoyniak, C. P., Tillman, R., Barch, D. M., & Luby, J. (2021). Callous-Unemotional Traits as an Intervention Target and Moderator of Parent-Child Interaction Therapy-Emotion Development Treatment for Preschool Depression and Conduct Problems. J*ournal of the American Academy of Child and Adolescent Psychiatry, 60*(11), 1394–1403. https://doi.org/10.1016/j.jaac.2021.03.018

Ebrahimi, A., Athar, M. E., Bakhshizadeh, M., Lavasani, F. F., & Andershed, H. (2022). The Persian version of the youth psychopathic traits inventory-short version (YPI-S): a psychometric evaluation. *Bulletin of the Menninger Clinic, 86*(1), 48-66. https://doi.org/10.1521/bumc.2022.86.1.48

Edens, J. E., Marcus, D., & Vaughn, M. G. (2011). Exploring the taxometric status of psychopathy among youthful offenders: Is there a juvenile psychopath taxon? *Law and Human Behavior, 35*, 13–24.

Egger, G., Liang, G., Aparicio, A., & Jones, P. A. (2004). Epigenetics in human disease and prospects for epigenetic therapy. *Nature, 429*(6990), 457-463.

Elkind, D. (1967). Egocentrism in Adolescence. *Child Development, 38*(4), 1025–1034. https://doi.org/10.2307/1127100

Fanti, K. A., Demetriou, C. A., & Kimonis, E. R. (2013). Variants of callous-unemotional conduct problems in a community sample of adolescents. *Journal of Youth and Adolescence, 42*, 964–979.

Fazel, S., Burghart, M., Fanshawe, T., Gil, S. D., Monahan, J., & Yu, R. (2022). The predictive performance of criminal risk assessment tools used at sentencing: Systematic review of validation studies. *Journal of Criminal Justice*, *81*, 101902. https://doi.org/10.1016/j.jcrimjus.2022.101902

Fazel, S., Singh, J. P., Doll, H., & Grann, M. (2012). Use of risk assessment instruments to predict violence and antisocial behaviour in 73 samples involving 24 827 people: systematic review and meta-analysis. *British Medical Journal*, *345*, e4692 (12 pages).

Felitti, V. J., Anda, R. F., Nordenberg, D., Williamson, D. F., Spitz, A. M., Edwards, V., Koss, M. P., & Marks, J. S. (1998). Relationship of childhood abuse and household dysfunction to many of the leading causes of death in adults: The Adverse Childhood Experiences (ACE) Study. *American Journal of Preventive Medicine, 14*(4), 245–258. https://doi.org/10.1016/S0749-3797(98)00017-8 https://www.ajpmonline.org/action/showPdf?pii=S0749-3797%2898%2900017-8

Fleming, G. E., Neo, B., Briggs, N. E., Kaouar, S., Frick, P. J., & Kimonis, E. R. (2022). Parent Training Adapted to the Needs of Children With Callous-Unemotional Traits: A Randomized Controlled Trial. *Behavior Therapy*, *53*(6), 1265–1281. https://doi.org/10.1016/j.beth.2022.07.001

Flexon, J. L. (2015). Evaluating Variant Callous–Unemotional Traits among Non-Institutionalized Youth: Implications for Violence Research and Policy. *Youth Violence and Juvenile Justice, 13*, 18-40.

Flexon, J. L. (2016). Callous-Unemotional Traits and Differently Motivated Aggression: An Examination of Variants in a Noninstitutionalized Sample. *Youth Violence and Juvenile Justice, 14*(4), 367–389.

Flexon, J. L., & Encalada, T. M. (2020). Antecedents to Secondary-Like Psychopathy in Noninstitutionalized Youth. *The Journal of Forensic Psychiatry & Psychology, 32*(4), 535–559. https://doi.org/10.1080/14789949.2020.1867620

Flexon, J. L., & Meldrum, R. C. (2013). Adolescent psychopathy and juvenile delinquency: Additive and nonadditive effects with key criminological variables. *Youth Violence and Juvenile Justice, 11*, 348–368.

Forth, A. E., Kosson, D. S., & Hare, R. D. (2003). *Hare Psychopathy Checklist: Youth Version (PCL-YV) technical manual*. Multi-Health Systems.

Frick, P. J., & Ray, J. V. (2015). Evaluating callous-unemotional traits as a personality construct. *Journal of Personality, 83*(6), 710-722.

Frick, P. J., Ray, J. V., Thornton, L. C., & Kahn, R. E. (2014). Can callous-unemotional traits enhance the understanding, diagnosis, and treatment of serious conduct problems in children and adolescents? A comprehensive review. *Psychological Bulletin, 140*(1), 1-57.

Gao, Y., & Raine, A. (2010). Successful and unsuccessful psychopaths: A neurobiological model. *Behavioral Sciences & the Law, 28*(2), 194-210.

Gillett, G., & Tamatea, A. J. (2012). The warrior gene: epigenetic considerations. *New Genetics and Society, 31*(1), 41-53.

Glenn, A. L., & Raine, A. (2014). *Psychopathy: An introduction to biological findings and their implications*. New York: New York University Press.

Glueck, S., & Glueck, E. (1950). *Unraveling juvenile delinquency*.

New York, NY: Commonwealth Fund.

Gottfredson, M., & Hirschi, T. (1990). A general theory of crime. Palo Alto, CA: Stanford University Press.

Gray, P., Smithson, H., & Jump, D. (2021). Serious youth violence and its relationship with adverse childhood experiences, HM Inspectorate of Probation Academic Insights 2021/13. *Manchester: HM Inspectorate of Probation.*

https://www.justiceinspectorates.gov.uk/hmiprobation/wp-content/uploads/sites/5/2021/11/Academic-Insights-Gray-et-al.pdf

Gunter, T. D., Vaughn, M. G., & Philibert, R. A. (2010). Behavioral genetics in antisocial spectrum disorders and psychopathy: A review of the recent literature. *Behavioral Sciences & the Law, 28*(2), 148-173.

Hare, R. D. (1991). *The Hare psychopathy checklist-revised (PCL-R).* Toronto, ON: Multi-Health Systems.

Hare, R. D. (2003). *The Hare psychopathy checklist-revised. 2nd ed.* Multi-Health Systems.

Hare, R. D. (2016). Psychopathy, the PCL-R, and criminal justice: Some new findings and current issues. *Canadian Psychology/Psychologie Canadienne, 57*(1), 21-34.

Hare, R. D., & Neumann, C. S. (2005). The structure of psychopathy. *Current Psychiatry Reports, 7*, 1–32.

Hare, R. D., & Neumann, C. (2010). The role of antisociality in the psychopathy construct: Comment on Skeem and Cooke (2010). *Psychological Assessment, 22*, 446–454.

Harpur, T. J., Hare, R. D., & Hakstian, A. R. (1989). Two-factor conceptualizations of psychopathy: Construct validity and assessment implications. *Psychological Assessment: A journal of Counseling and Clinical Assessment*, *1*, 6–17.

Harris, A. J. R., Phenix, A., Hanson, R.K., & Thornton, D. (2003). *Static-99 coding rules: revised 2003*. Solicitor General Canada.

Harris, G. T., & Rice, M. E. (2006). *Treatment of psychopathy: A review of empirical findings*. In C. J. Patrick (Ed.), Handbook of psychopathy. (pp. 555–572). New York: Guilford.

Harvard Law Review. (2025). *Psychopathy and capital sentencing*. Harvard Law Review, 138(4), 1101–1123. https://harvardlawreview.org/print/vol-138/bias-baked-in-how-antisocial-personality-disorder-diagnoses-trigger-legal-failure/

Hay, C., Fortson, E. N., Hollist, D. R., Altheimer, I., & Schaible, L. M. (2006). The impact of community disadvantage on the relationship between the family and juvenile crime. *Journal of Research in Crime and Delinquency*, *43*, 326–356.

Hawes, S. W., Mulvey, E. P., Schubert, C. A., & Pardini, D. A. (2014). Structural coherence and temporal stability of psychopathic personality features during emerging adulthood. *Journal of Abnormal Psychology*, *123*(3), 623-633.

Heijmans B. T., Tobi E. L., Stein A. D., Putter H., Blauw G. J., Susser E.S., Slagboom P. E., & Lumeye L.H. (2008). Persistent epigenetic differences associated with prenatal exposure to famine in humans. *Proc Natl Acad Sci USA, 05*(44), 17046–17049.

Hirschi, T. (1969). *Causes of delinquency*. Berkeley, CA: University of California Press.

Hoeve, M., Dubas, J. S., Eichelsheim, V. I., van der Laan, P. H., Smeenk, W., & Gerris, J. R. M. (2009). The relationship between parenting and delinquency: A meta-analysis. *Journal of Abnormal Child Psychology, 37,* 749–775.

Howard, A. L., Kimonis, E. R., Muñoz, L. C., & Frick, P. J. (2012). Violence exposure mediates the relation between callous-unemotional traits and offending patterns in adolescents. *Journal of Abnormal Child Psychology, 40,* 1237–1247.

Jackson, D.B., Jones, M.S., Semenza, D.C., & Testa, A. (2023). Adverse Childhood Experiences and Adolescent Delinquency: A Theoretically Informed Investigation of Mediators during Middle Childhood. *Int J Environ Res Public Health, 11*;20(4):3202. doi: 10.3390/ijerph20043202. PMID: 36833897; PMCID: PMC9959059.

https://www.mdpi.com/1660-4601/20/4/3202

Jirtle R. L., & Skinner M. K. (2007). Environmental epigenomics and disease susceptibility. *Nature Reviews Genetics, 8,* 253-262.

Karpman, B. (1941). On the need of separating psychopathy into two distinct clinical types: The symptomatic and the idiopathic. *Journal of Criminal Psychopathology, 3,* 112–137.

Karpman, B. (1948). The myth of the psychopathic personality. *American Journal of Psychiatry, 104,* 523–534.

Kelly, D. H., & Pink, W. T. (1972-1973). School commitment, youth rebellion, and delinquency. *Criminology, 10,* 473–485.

Kerig, P. K., Bennett, D. C., Thompson, M., & Becker, S. P. (2012). Nothing really matters: Emotional numbing as a link between trauma exposure and callousness in delinquent youth. *Journal of Traumatic*

Stress, *25*(3), 272-279.

Kimonis, E. R., Cross, B., Howard, A., & Donoghue, K. (2013). Maternal care, maltreatment and callous-unemotional traits among urban male juvenile offenders. *Journal of youth and adolescence*, *42*(2), 165-177.

Kimonis, E. R., Fanti, K. A., Isoma, Z., & Donoghue, K. (2013). Maltreatment profiles among incarcerated boys with callous-unemotional traits. *Child Maltreatment, 18,* 108–121.

Kimonis, E. R., Frick, P. J., & Barry, C. T. (2004). Callous-unemotional traits and delinquent peer affiliation. *Journal of Counseling and Clinical Psychology, 72,* 956–966.

Kimonis, E. R., Skeem, J. L., Cauffman, E., & Dmitrieva, J. (2011). Are secondary variants of juvenile psychopathy more reactively violent and less psychosocially mature than primary variants. *Law and Human Behavior, 35,* 381–391.

Kosson, D. S., & Newman, J. (1995). An evaluation of Mealy's hypotheses based on psychopathy checklist identified groups. *Behavioral and Brain Sciences, 18,* 562–563.

Kosson, D. S., Smith, S. S., & Newman, J. P. (1990). Evaluation of the construct validity of psychopathy in Black and White male inmates: Three preliminary studies. *Journal of Abnormal Psychology, 99,* 250-259.

Kropp, P.R., Hart, S.D., Webster, C.D., & Eaves, D. (1994). *Manual for the spousal assault risk assessment guide.* British Columbia Institute on Family Violence.

Kropp, P.R., Hart, S.D., Webster, C.D., & Eaves, D. (1995). *Manual for the spousal assault risk assessment guide. 2nd ed.* British Columbia Institute on Family Violence.

Kropp, P.R., Hart, S.D., Webster, C.D., & Eaves, D. (1999). *Spousal assault risk assessment guide (SARA).* Multi-Health Systems.

Larsson, H., Andershed, H., & Lichtenstein, P. (2006). A genetic factor explains most of the variation in the psychopathic personality. *Journal of Abnormal Psychology, 115*, 221–230.

Leistico, A. M. R., Salekin, R. T., DeCoster, J., & Rogers, R. (2008). A large-scale meta-analysis relating the Hare measures of psychopathy to anti-social conduct. *Law and Human Behavior, 32*(1), 28-45.

Levenson, M. R., Kiehl, K. A., & Fitzpatrick, C. M. (1995). Assessing psychopathic attributes in a noninstitutionalized population. *Journal of Personality and Social Psychology, 68*(1), 151–158. https://doi.org/10.1037/0022-3514.68.1.151

Lilienfeld, S. O., & Andrews, B. P. (1996). Development and preliminary validation of a self-report measure of psychopathic personality traits in noncriminal populations. *Journal of Personality Assessment, 66*, 488–524.

Lilienfeld, S. O., & Hess, T. H. (2001). Psychopathic personality traits and somatization: Sex differences and the mediating role of negative emotionality. *Journal of Psychopathology and Behavioral Assessment, 23*, 11–24.

Lilienfeld, S. O., & Widows, M. (2005). *Professional manual for the psychopathic personality inventory-revised (PPI-R).* Lutz, FL: Psychological Assessment Resources.

Loney, B.R., Taylor, J., Butler, M.A., & Iacono, W.G. (2007). Adolescent psychopathy features: 6-year temporal stability and the prediction of externalizing symptoms during transition to adulthood. *Aggressive Behavior, 33*, 242-252.

Lynam, D. R. (1996). Early identification of chronic offenders: Who is the fledgling psychopath? *Psychological Bulletin, 120*, 209–234.

Lynam D. R. (1997). Pursuing the psychopath: Capturing the fledgling psychopath in the nomological net. *Journal of Abnormal Psychology, 106*, 425–438.

Lynam D. R. (1998). Early identification of the fledgling psychopath: Locating the psychopathic child in the current nomenclature. *Journal of Abnormal Psychology, 107*, 566–575.

Lynam, D. R., Caspi, A., Moffitt, T. E., Loeber, R., & Stouthamer-Loeber, M. (2007). Longitudinal evidence that psychopathy scores in early adolescence predict adult psychopathy. *Journal of Abnormal Psychology, 116*, 155–165.

Lynam, D. R., Gaughan, E. T., Miller, J. D., Miller, D. J., Mullins-Sweatt, S., & Widiger, T. A. (2011). Assessing the basic traits associated with psychopathy: Development and validation of the Elemental Psychopathy Assessment. *Psychological Assesment, 23*(1), 108-124.

Lynam, D. R., & Gudonis, L. (2005). The development of psychopathy. *Annual Review of Clinical Psychology, 1*, 381–407.

Lynam, D. R., Loeber, R., & Stouthamer-Loeber, M. (2008). The stability of psychopathy from adolescence into adulthood: The search for moderators. *Criminal Justice and Behavior, 35*(2), 228-243.

Matz, A. K., Martinez, A. R., & Kujava, E. (2021). Assessing Risk in North Dakota Juvenile Probation: A Preliminary Examination of the

Predictive Validity of the Youth Assessment and Screening Instrument. *Crime & Delinquency*, *67*(4), 551-573. https://doi.org/10.1177/0011128720950023

Međedović, J. (2024). Observing psychopathy promptly, reliably, and validly: Development and validation of the Short Psychopathy Rating Scale (SPRS). *Personality and Individual Differences*, *219*, 112520. https://doi.org/10.1016/j.paid.2023.112520

Meier, M. H., Slutske, W. S., Arndt, S., & Cadoret, R. L. (2008). Impulsive and callous traits are more strongly associated with delinquent behavior in higher risk neighborhoods among boys and girls. *Journal of Abnormal Psychology*, *117*, 377–385.

Michonski, J. D., & Sharp, C. (2010). Revisiting Lynam's notion of the ''Fledgling Psychopath'': Are HIA-CP children truly psychopathic-like? *Child and Adolescent Psychiatry and Mental Health, 4*, 1–9.

Mitchell, T., E., Wormith, S. J., & Tafrate, R. C. (2016). Implications of risk-need-responsivity principles for forensic CBT. *The Behavior Therapist, 39*, 147-153.

Morse, S. J. (2008). Psychopathy and criminal responsibility. *Neuroethics*, *1*(3), 205-212.

Muris, P., Mayer, B., Reinders, E., & Wesenhagen, C. (2011). Person-related protective and vulnerability factors of psychopathology symptoms in non-clinical adolescents. *Community Mental Health Journal*, *47*, 47–60.

Murrie, D. C., Marcus, D. K., Douglas, K. S., Lee, Z., Salekin, R. T., & Vincent, G. (2007). Youth with psychopathic features are not a discrete class: A taxometric analysis. *Journal of Child Psychology and*

Psychiatry, 48, 714–723.

Oba, T., Katahira, K., Kimura, K., & Takano, K. (2024). A network analysis on psychopathy and theoretically relevant personality traits. *Personality and Individual Differences, 217,* 112437. https://doi.org/10.1016/j.paid.2023.112437

Orbis Partners, Inc. (2007). *Youth Assessment and Screening Instrument: Technical manual.* Orbis Partners.

Patrick, C. J. (2022). Psychopathy: Current knowledge and future directions. *Annual Review of Clinical Psychology, 18*(1), 387-415. https://doi.org/10.1146/annurev-clinpsy-072720-012851

Pauli-Pott, U., Sens, L., & Pott, C. (2025). Association between callous unemotional traits cognitive control performance and reward sensitivity in youths with conduct problems–A systematic review and meta-analysis. *Neuroscience & Biobehavioral Reviews,* 106211. https://doi.org/10.1016/j.neubiorev.2025.106211

Pisano, S., & Masi, G. (2020). Recommendations for the pharmacological management of irritability and aggression in conduct disorder patients. *Expert Opinion on Pharmacotherapy, 21*(1), 5-7. https://doi.org/10.1080/14656566.2019.1685498

Porter, S. (1996). Without conscience or without active conscience? The etiology of psychopathy revisited. *Aggression and Violent Behavior, 1,* 179–189.

Pratt, T. C., & Cullen, F. T. (2000). The empirical status of Gottfredson and Hirschi's general theory of crime: A meta-analysis. *Criminology, 38,* 931–964.

Pratt, T. C., Cullen, F. T., Sellers, C. S., Winfree, Jr., L. T., & Madensen, T. D., Daigle, L. E., Fearn, N. E., & Gau, J. M. (2010). The empirical status of social learning theory: A meta-analysis. *Justice Quarterly, 27*, 765–802.

Painter R. C., Roseboom T. J., & Bleker O. P. (2005). Prenatal exposure to the Dutch famine and disease in later life: an overview. *Reproductive Toxicology, 20*, 345-352.

Quinsey V. L. (1998). Harris GT, Rice ME, Cormier CA. *Violent offenders: appraising and managing risk.* American Psychological Association.

Quinsey V. L. (2006). Harris GT, Rice ME, Cormier CA. *Violent offenders: appraising and managing risk. 2nd ed.* American Psychological Association.

Robins, L. (1966). *Deviant children grown up: A sociological and psychiatric study of sociopathic personality.* Baltimore, MD: Williams and Wilkins.

Roper v. Simmons, 543 U.S. 551.

Salekin, R. T. (2002). Psychopathy and therapeutic pessimism: Clinical lore or clinical reality. *Clinical Psychology Review, 22*, 79–112.

Salekin, R. T. (2008). Psychopathy and recidivism from mid-adolescence to young adulthood: Cumulating legal problems and limiting life opportunities. *Journal of Abnormal Psychology, 117*, 386–395.

Salekin, R. T. (2017). Research Review: What do we know about psychopathic traits in children. *The Journal of Child Psychology and Psychiatry, 58*(11), 1180-1200.

Salekin, R. T., & Frick, P. J. (2005). Psychopathy in children and adolescents: The need for a developmental perspective. *Journal of Ab-*

normal Child Psychology, *33*, 403–409.

Salekin, T., Worley, C., & Grimes, R. D. (2010). Treatment of psychopathy: A review and brief introduction to the model approach for psychopathy. *Behavioral Sciences and the Law*, *28*, 235–266.

Salekin, R. T., Tippey, J. G., & Allen, A. D. (2012). Treatment of conduct problem youth with interpersonal callous traits using mental models: Measurement of risk and change. *Behavioral Sciences and the Law, 30*, 470–486.

Salekin, R. T., Neumann, C. S., Leistico, A. R., DiCicco, T. M., & Duro, R. L. (2004). Psychopathy and comorbidity in a young offender sample: Taking a closer look at psychopathy's potential importance over disruptive behavior disorders. *Journal of Abnormal Psychology*, *113*, 416–427.

Sanz-García, A., Gesteira, C., Sanz, J., & García-Vera, M. P. (2021). Prevalence of psychopathy in the general adult population: A systematic review and meta-analysis. *Frontiers in Psychology*, *12*, 661044. https://doi.org/10.3389/fpsyg.2021.661044

Seagrave, D., & Grisso, T. (2002). Adolescent development and the measurement of juvenile psychopathy. *Law and Human Behavior*, *26*(2), 219-239.

Schaarsberg, R. E. K., Ribberink, A. Z., Osinga, B., van Dam, L., Lindauer, R. J., & Popma, A. (2023). Treatment responsivity in adolescents with disruptive behavior problems: co-creation of a virtual reality–based add-on intervention. *JMIR Formative Research*, *7*(1), e46592.

Skeem, J. L., & Cooke, D. J. (2010a). Is criminal behavior a central component of psychopathy? Conceptual directions for resolving the debate. *Psychological Assessment, 22*(2), 433-445.

Skeem, J. L., & Cooke, D. J., (2010b). One measure does not a construct make: Directions toward reinvigorating psychopathy research – A reply to Hare and Neumann (2010). *Psychological Assessment, 22*, 455–459.

Skeem, J. L., Johansson, P., Andershed, H., Kerr, M., & Louden, J. E. (2007). Two subtypes of psychopathic violent offenders that parallel primary and secondary variants. *Journal of Abnormal Psychology, 116(2)*, 395–409.

Skeem, J. L., Poythress, N., Edens, J. F., Lilienfeld, S. O., & Cale, E. M. (2003). Psychopathic personality or personalities? Exploring potential variants of psychopathy and their implications for risk assessment. *Aggression and Violent Behavior, 8*(5), 513-546.

Smith, S. T., Edens, J. F., Clark, J., & Rulseh, A. (2014). "So, what is a psychopath?" Venireperson perceptions, beliefs, and attitudes about psychopathic personality. *Law and Human Behavior, 38*(5), 490-500.

Stolzenberg, L., & D'Alessio, S. J. (2008). Co-Offending and the Age-Crime Curve. *Journal of Research in Crime and Delinquency, 45*(1), 65-86. https://doi.org/10.1177/0022427807309441

Tamatea, A. J. (2015). 'Biologizing' Psychopathy: Ethical, Legal, and Research Implications at the Interface of Epigenetics and Chronic Antisocial Conduct. *Behavioral Sciences & the Law, 33*(5), 629-643.

Taubner, S., Hauschild, S., Kasper, L., Kaess, M., Sobanski, E., Gablonski, T. C., ... & Volkert, J. (2021). Mentalization-based treatment for adolescents with conduct disorder (MBT-CD): protocol of a feasibility and pilot study. *Pilot and Feasibility Studies, 7*(1), 139. https://doi.org/10.1186/s40814-021-00876-2

Teixeira, E. H., Celeri, E. V., Jacintho, A. C., & Dalgalarrondo, P. (2013). Clozapine in severe conduct disorder. *Journal of Child and Adolescent Psychopharmacology, 23*(1), 44-48.

Thomson, N. D., Kevorkian, S. S., Hazlett, L., Perera, R., & Vrana, S. (2025). A new treatment approach to conduct disorder and callous-unemotional traits: an assessment of the acceptability, appropriateness, and feasibility of Impact VR. *Frontiers in psychiatry, 16*, 1484938. https://doi.org/10.3389/fpsyt.2025.1484938

Thomson, N. D., Perera, R. A., Kevorkian, S. S., Hazlett, L., & Vrana, S. (2025). Impact VR: A Socioemotional Intervention for Reducing CU Traits, Conduct Problems, and Aggression in Youth with Conduct Disorder. *Research on Child and Adolescent Psychopathology*, 1-14. https://doi.org/10.1007/s10802-025-01373-3

Thornberry, T. P. (1987). Toward and Interactional Theory of Delinquency. *Criminology, 25*, 863–891.

Thornberry, T. P., Lizotte, A. J., Krohn, M., Farnworth, M., & Joon Jang, S. (1991). Testing interactional theory: An examination of reciprocal casual relationships among family, school and delinquency. *Journal of Criminal Law and Criminology, 82*, 3–35.

van Os, J., & Selten, J. P. (1998). Prenatal exposure to maternal stress and subsequent schizophrenia. The May 1940 invasion of The Netherlands. *British Journal of Psychiatry, 172*, 324-326.

Vaughn, M. G., & DeLisi, M. (2008). Were Wolfgang's chronic offenders psychopaths? On the convergent validity between psychopathy and career criminality. *Journal of Criminal Justice, 36*, 33–42.

Vaughn, M. G., DeLisi, M., Beaver, K. M., & Wright, J. P. (2009). Identifying latent classes of behavioral risk based on early childhood:

Manifestations of self-control. *Youth Violence and Juvenile Justice*, 7, 16–31.

Vaughn, M. G., DeLisi, M., Beaver, K. M., Wright, J. P., & Howard, M.O. (2007). Toward a psychopathology of self-control theory: The importance of narcissistic traits. *Behavioral Sciences and the Law*, 25, 803–821.

Vaughn, M. G., Edens, J. F., Howard, M. O., & Smith, S. T. (2009). An investigation of primary and secondary psychopathy in a statewide sample of incarcerated youth. *Youth Violence and Juvenile Justice*, 7, 172–188.

Vaughn, M. G., & Howard, M. O. (2005). The construct of psychopathy and its potential contribution to the study of serious, violent, and chronic offending. *Youth Violence and Juvenile Justice*, 3, 235–252.

Vaughn, M. G., Howard, M. O., & DeLisi, M. (2008). Psychopathic personality traits and delinquent careers: An empirical examination. *International Journal of Law and Psychiatry*, 31, 407–416.

Vaughn, M. G., Litschge, C., DeLisi, M., Beaver, K. M., & McMillen, C. J. (2008). Psychopathic personality features and risks for criminal justice system involvement among emancipating foster youth. *Children and Youth Services Review*, 30, 1101–1110.

Vachon, D. D., Lynam, D. R., Loeber, R., & Stouthamer-Loeber, M. (2012). Generalizing the nomological network of psychopathy across populations differing on race and conviction status. *Journal of Abnormal Psychology*, 121(1), 263-269.

Veal, R., & Ogloff, J. R. P. (2022). The concept of psychopathy and risk assessment: Historical developments, contemporary considerations, and future directions. In P. B. Marques, M. Paulino, & L. Alho

(Eds.), *Psychopathy and criminal behavior* (pp. 169–192). Academic Press. https://doi.org/10.1016/B978-0-12-811419-3.00011-X

Viding, E. R., Blair, J., Moffit, T. E., & Plomin, R. (2005). Evidence for substantial genetic risk for psychopathy in 7-year-olds. Journal of Child Psychology and Psychiatry, *46*, 592–597.

Viljoen, J. L., Cochrane, D. M., & Jonnson, M. R. (2018). Do risk assessment tools help manage and reduce risk of violence and reoffending? A systematic review. *Law and Human Behavior, 42*(3), 181–214. https://doi.org/10.1037/lhb0000280

Webster, C. D., Eaves, D., Douglas, K. S., & Wintrup, A. (1995). *The HCR-20 scheme: the assessment of dangerousness and risk.* Forensic Psychiatric Services Commission of British Columbia.

Webster, C. D., Douglas, K. S., Eaves, D., & Hart, S.D. (1997). *HCR-20: assessing risk for violence (version 2).* Simon Fraser University, Mental Health, Law, and Policy Institute.

Weibe, R. (2003). Reconciling psychopathy and low self-control. *Justice Quarterly, 20*, 297–336.

Weisz, J. R., & Stipek, D. J. (1982). Competence, contingency, and the development of perceived control. *Human Development, 25*, 250–281.

White, B. A., Olver, M. E., & Lilienfeld, S. O. (2016). Psychopathy: Its relevance, nature, assessment, and treatment. *The Behavior Therapist, 39*, 154-161.

Wootton, B. (1959). *Social science and social pathology.* New York: Macmillan.

Zagórski, K., Kozik, M., Skalska-Dziobek, N., Małagocka, W., Chybowska, K., Naruszewicz, M., & Cetnarowski, P. (2025). Treatment of aggression in conduct disorders in children and adolescents. *Quality in Sport*, *39*, 58998. https://doi.org/10.12775/QS.2025.39.58998

Legal Cases

Carter v. State, 212 N.W. 614 (Neb. 1927).

Matter of State of New York v. Anthony L., 57 Misc. 3d 1222(A), 2017 N.Y. Slip Op. 51375(U) (Sup. Ct. Kings Cty. 2017).

Matter of State of New York v. Dennis K. (2010/2011) Matter of State of New York v. Dennis K., 27 Misc. 3d 1202(A), 2010 N.Y. Slip Op. 50547(U) (Sup. Ct. N.Y. County 2010).

Matter of State of New York v. Kareem M. (2018) Matter of State of New York v. Kareem M., 62 Misc. 3d 1203(A), 2018 N.Y. Slip Op. 52044(U) (Sup. Ct. Bronx Cty. 2018).

Kansas v. Hendricks, 521 U.S. 346 (1997).

Roper v. Simmons, 543 U.S. 551 (2005).

ABOUT THE AUTHOR

Jamie L. Flexon is a professor of criminology and criminal justice in the School of International and Public Affairs at Florida International University. Her M.A. and Ph.D. were earned at the School of Criminal Justice, University at Albany in Albany, New York.

Her research interests involve juvenile delinquency, juvenile psychopathy, criminal justice issues related to punishment, and policy evaluation. She has presented numerous papers at professional conferences, and her research has appeared in various outlets, including *Journal of Criminal Justice, Crime & Delinquency, Journal of Quantitative Criminology, Criminal Justice and Behavior, American Journal of Criminal Justice, International Journal of Offender Therapy and Comparative Criminology, Youth Violence and Juvenile Justice, Victims & Offenders, Journal of Studies on Alcohol and Drugs,* among others. Dr. Flexon also is the author of the book, *Racial Disparities in Capital Sentencing: Prejudice and Discrimination in the Jury Room* (2012), as well as others, and a contributing author to chapters in books, such as *Wrongly Convicted, Perspectives on Failed Justice* and *Race and the Death Penalty: The Legacy of McCleskey v. Kemp.*

Dr. Flexon is a member of the American Society of Criminology (ASC), The Academy of Criminal Justice Sciences (ACJS), and the Southern Criminal Justice Association. Belonging to the American Bar Association (ABA) and the Criminal Justice Section of the ABA, Dr. Flexon has served on a number of committees including the Juvenile Justice Committee, Forensic & Investigative Practices Committee, and the Science Technology & Forensics Committee of the ABA. She also reviews for various journals, as well as for publishing companies, and serves as an editorial board member for top journals in the field.